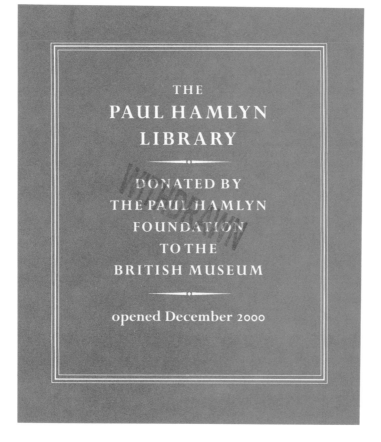

LIBRARY OF AMERICAN
INDIAN HISTORY

WOUNDED KNEE 1890

The End of the Plains Indian Wars

Tom Streissguth

Facts On File, Inc.

ACKNOWLEDGMENTS

Thanks to Mike Conner, Marian Streissguth, John Simmons, Harold and Barbara High Pine, Vince Twoeagles, J. S. Dill, Nicole Bowen, the Minnesota Historical Society, and the South Dakota State Historical Society for their help in preparing this book.

Wounded Knee 1890: The End of the Plains Indian Wars

Facts On File, Inc.
11 Penn Plaza
New York NY 10001

Library of Congress Cataloging-in-Publication Data

Streissguth, Thomas, 1958–
    Wounded Knee 1890 : the end of the Plains Indian wars / by Tom Streissguth.
      p. cm.—(Library of American Indian history)
    Includes bibliographical references and index.
    Summary: Narrates the events leading up to the massacre which marked the end of a long succession of wars between whites and Indians, and concludes with a description of the battle itself.
    ISBN 0-8160-3600-4
    1. Wounded Knee Massacre, S.D., 1890—Juvenile literature. 2. Dakota Indians—Wars, 1890–1891—Juvenile literature. 3. Dakota Indians—Government relations—Juvenile literature. [1. Wounded Knee Massacre, S.D., 1890. 2. Dakota Indians—Wars, 1890–1891. 3. Dakota Indians—Government relations.] I. Title. II. Series.
E83.89.S77 1998
973.8′6—dc21   97-43530

Text design by Cathy Rincon
Cover design by Amy Beth Gonzalez
Illustrations on pages 19, 28, 51, and 84 by Jeremy Eagle

Printed in the United States of America

MP FOF 10 9 8 7 6 5 4 3 2 1

This book is printed on acid-free paper.

CONTENTS

▲

INTRODUCTION

In the late afternoon of December 28, 1890, a squadron of the U.S. Seventh Cavalry formed up at the Pine Ridge Agency, on the Pine Ridge Indian Reservation. The squadron commander, Colonel James Forsyth, had orders to lead his troops about 15 miles to the northeast and assist another squadron of the Seventh, under Major Samuel Whitside, in the disarmament of a band of Miniconjou Lakota Indians. The disarmament would take place the next morning; Forsyth, Whitside, and their commanders, Brigadier General John Brooke and General Nelson Miles, expected it to bring a swift, peaceful end to the recent conflict known as the Ghost Dance War. Later in the evening, Forsyth's men reached their destination in sight of the Lakota, who were camping under a white flag on a small plain just west of Wounded Knee Creek.

The massacre that would take place the next morning marked the end of the long and sporadic war between whites and Indians on the Great Plains of North America. The conflict began in the early 1700s, when the first European explorers, soldiers, and fur trappers were crossing the Mississippi River and following the river's western tributaries. These Europeans traveled lands no white person had ever seen; seeing them nearly uninhabited, and uncivilized, they claimed these lands in the names of their kings and their companies. At the small trading posts that they built on the rivers, they exchanged their own supplies for fur pelts brought to them by the scattered bands of Plains Indians. Until the early 19th century, the English, French, and Spanish carried on a rivalry for land and resources in the center of the new continent. In the 1800s, the European nations would be pushed aside by the United States.

While the fur trappers moved west, another great migration took place in the same country. The Dakota (known as the "Sioux" to their enemies, the Ojibwa, and to the whites) were leaving the northern forests and settling on the Great Plains. With only war clubs and arrows to match the guns owned by the Ojibwa, the Dakota fled the upper Mississippi region and journeyed south and west, toward the valley of the Minnesota River. The Santee Dakota remained in this valley and in the surrounding prairies. The Teton, another main division of the Dakota, continued westward, to the open plains that reached 200 miles to the east and west of the Missouri River.

The change of land brought a complete change in lifestyle. The Teton, who called themselves Lakota, had once lived by hunting small game and by gathering roots and berries. In the forest, they had moved on foot and had lived in permanent homes of bark and earth. Now, using horses captured or bought from other tribes, they hunted the huge buffalo herds of the Great Plains for their meat and clothing. They became nomads, following the herds as they migrated north in the spring and south in the fall. Deer and antelope were plentiful; there was a sea of grass for the horses, and small bands of white traders available for the necessary supplies and tools: awls, beads, blankets, knives, needles, and guns. The Lakota raised tipis made of long, straight lodgepoles and covered with buffalo hides. The tipis could be quickly taken down and easily moved; they provided a more practical shelter for a people who had adopted an entirely new life as nomadic hunters.

The Dakota soon made the northern Great Plains, from the Minnesota River valley west to the foothills of the Rocky Mountains, their homeland. They drove out the Arikara, Mandan, Crow, and other tribes of the upper Missouri River valley. By 1800,

As the Dakota moved onto the Great Plains, buffalo became their main source of food. *(Watercolor by Peter Rindisbacher. From the Minnesota Historical Society)*

they controlled traffic on the great river. Wrote Dr. Charles A. Eastman, a Santee who lived in both the white and Indian worlds:

> The Sioux roamed over an area nearly a thousand miles in extent. In the summer we gathered together in large numbers, but towards fall we would divide into small groups or bands and scatter for the trapping and the winter hunt. Most of us hugged the wooded river bottoms; some depended entirely upon the buffalo for food, while others, and among those my immediate kindred, hunted all kinds of game, and trapped and fished as well.

Among the Lakota, there were seven main divisions. The Miniconjou, Sans Arc (Itazipco), Oohenonpa, Sihasapa, and Hunkpapa, made up a northern branch that migrated west from Big Stone Lake and the headwaters of the Minnesota River. The Brulé and Oglala occupied lands farther south. The Oglala settled along the Bad River, which empties into the Missouri near the city of Pierre, and the Brulé along the White River, which winds through the dry plains lying south of the Badlands. Oglala and Brulé hunting parties ranged as far west as the Big Horn Mountains and as far south as the plains of Kansas, beyond the Platte River.

The land of the Lakota was dry and nearly treeless. In winter, fierce blizzards blew across the bare hills; the summer's hot winds burned up the grass. But in 1775, a war party led by the Oglala chief Standing Bull discovered a region of mountains, cool streams, plentiful game, and a mild climate. This paradise lay directly west of the lands where the Oglala and Brulé roamed. It was a home given them by *Wakan Tanka*: the Great Spirit, and it was given the name of *Paha Sapa*: the Black Hills. The Lakota soon drove the Kiowa and Crow from the Black Hills and claimed them as a sacred homeland, never to be surrendered.

A century later, however, the Black Hills would be given up—to a land-hungry nation of white people who were moving westward faster and in far greater numbers than any group of Indians. The Lakota first encountered these people in the summer of 1804, when a well-armed group of soldiers and guides rowed up the Missouri River in three boats. These men had come neither to fight nor to trade. Instead, they landed near the mouth of the Bad River to shake hands with the Lakota chiefs, to raise a striped flag, and to make a long speech. Dressed in a fine blue uniform, the chief of these men explained that the country all around, the country of the Lakota, was now the property of a powerful but kind and just Great Father who lived in a big city far to the east.

Disappointed by the meager presents brought by the white men, the Lakota nearly decided to kill them. Weapons were raised on both sides; the white men took aim at a group of Lakota warriors with a powerful cannon mounted on one of the boats. But the meeting ended peacefully, and the boats proceeded on their way north. That winter, Meriwether Lewis, William Clark, and their Corps of Discovery stopped at the villages of the Mandan on the upper Missouri. Clark reported the following about the Lakota he had met at the Bad River (who he called the Teton):

> . . . the Sioux possess the south west of the Missouri, above White river; 132 miles higher, and on the west side—Teton river falls into it, it is small, and heads in the open plains; here we met a large band of Sioux and the second which we had seen called Tetons, those are

great rascals, and may be justly termed the pirates of the Missouri; they made two attempts to stop us; they are subdivided and stretched on the river to near this place, having reduced the Ruaras [Arikara] and Mandans, and drove them from the country they now occupy . . .

Among the Missouri River fur traders and among their rival Indian tribes, the Lakota already had a reputation as fighters and pirates. But with the reports and diaries of Lewis and Clark, the Lakota gained further bad publicity in the United States. According to the two explorers sent up the Missouri by President Thomas Jefferson, these Indians were stubborn, treacherous, and well-armed. On Lewis's recommendation, the United States allied with the Lakota's enemies in order to open traffic on the river and to maintain a balance of power on the Great Plains.

But well after Lewis and Clark returned to the East, the Lakota kept their control of the Missouri River. They stopped traders, forcing some of them back downstream and others to give up their goods for meager compensation in beaver furs and buffalo hides. The Lakota flourished; their villages grew and their homeland remained secure against white or Indian enemies. But they now depended on the weapons and goods brought by white traders. Seeing that the two nations—Lakota and white—must somehow reach a permanent agreement, the United States decided to set down some conditions on a paper, to be signed by important men on both sides.

In 1825, the Lakota, as well as the Yankton and Yanktonai Dakota, signed their first treaty with a representative of the United States, Brigadier General Henry Atkinson. By the treaty's Article 1, "It is admitted by the Teton, Yankton, and Yanktonai bands of Sioux Indians, that they reside within the territorial limits of the United States, acknowledge their supremacy and claim their protection. The said bands also admit the right of the United States to regulate all intercourse and trade with them." In turn, the United States recognized the sovereignty of the Lakota over their own country around the Missouri River valley.

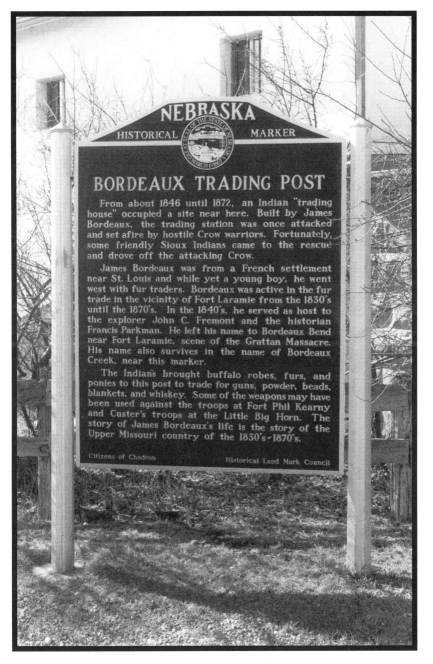

This marker in western Nebraska stands at the site of a 19th-century fur post. The Museum of the Fur Trade now occupies the site.   *(Photo by Tom Streissguth)*

The treaty was simple and straightforward. The United States believed it now had a monopoly on trade with the Dakota; the Lakota leaders saw their mastery of the northern Plains acknowledged by a weaker power. But the mutual understanding began to unravel starting in the 1830s, when a wave of westward migration and settlement began on the vast, open range of the Dakota Indians. White farmers had already settled the lower Missouri River, Minnesota, and Iowa. And despite the treaty provision that barred whites from their land, the Lakota saw the first westward migrants follow the Platte River along the Overland Trail in 1841. Starting from St. Louis and Independence, Missouri, these settlers were crossing the Great Plains and heading for Oregon and California. Their herds of cattle and horses, and the long trains of their heavy Conestoga wagons, left deep ruts that were easy to follow.

These white emigrants feared the hostile Lakota. Their fears were sharpened by book and newspaper accounts of battles and massacres on the frontier. The historian Francis Parkman, Jr., who journeyed through the land of the Lakota in 1846, reported that

> The Ogillallah, the Brulé, and the other western bands of Dakota or Sioux, are thorough savages, unchanged by any contact with civilization. Not one of them can speak a European tongue, or has ever visited an American settlement. Until within a year or two, when the emigrants began to pass through their country on the way to Oregon, they had seen no whites except the few employed about the Fur Company's posts.

The Lakota had their own good reasons to fear this westward migration. The whites passing through the Platte River valley left behind cholera, influenza, and measles, sicknesses against which Indians had no immunity. More wagon trails and trading posts were appearing in the country, and emigrants were slaughtering the buffalo by the hundreds and thousands. The vast herds, which the Lakota depended on for their food, winter clothing, and shelter, began to shrink and slowly disappear from the Plains.

In the late 1840s, the westward migration turned into a confrontation. Fearing violence between the emigrants and the Indians,

Thomas Fitzpatrick, a government Indian agent, recommended in a letter to Superintendant of Indian Affairs D. D. Mitchell that a treaty conference be held at Fort Laramie, an army post built on the Oregon Trail along the North Platte River. Fitzpatrick wanted to establish a legal right-of-way for the emigrants that would allow them to pass peacefully through the Great Plains. Mitchell agreed; in February 1851, the U.S. Congress approved the expenditure of $100,000 for the negotiations. Mitchell sent couriers to the Dakota, the Shoshone, the Crow, the Cheyenne, and other Plains tribes, promising generous presents to those chiefs who came to the treaty council. In September about 10,000 Indians assembled in the prairies and hills surrounding Fort Laramie.

That fall, Superintendant Mitchell reported from Fort Laramie:

> I . . . was much surprised to witness the sad change which
> a few years and unlooked-for circumstances had pro-
> duced. The buffalo, upon which [the Indians] rely for food,
> clothing, shelter, and traffic, are rapidly diminishing.
> The hordes of emigrants passing through the country
> seem to have scattered death and disease in all direc-
> tions. The tribes have suffered much from the small-pox
> and cholera, and perhaps still more from venereal diseases.

The leaders of the Lakota as well as Superintendant Mitchell wanted to end the troublesome contact between whites and Indians. They believed the Fort Laramie treaty would keep whites out of their lands, and they looked on the promised annuities (annual payments) as tribute, offered by the whites' government to them for the sake of peace.

So with little wrangling, the Fort Laramie treaty was concluded on September 17, 1851. For the first time, the U.S. government assigned an invisible boundary line to the Lakota, as well as to the Crow, Assiniboine, and other tribes present. The territory of the Lakota covered what is now North Dakota south of the Heart River, South Dakota west of the Missouri, northwestern Nebraska, and eastern Wyoming between the North Platte and the western slope of the Black Hills. The Indians agreed to allow white emigrants to traverse the Platte valley undisturbed. In addition,

SUPERINTENDANT MITCHELL'S REPORT CONCERNING THE FORT LARAMIE TREATY

For the U.S. government, one of the most difficult problems of the 19th century was how to fight, negotiate with, and subdue the American Indian. The Dakota, the largest and strongest Indian people of the Great Plains, posed the toughest problem of all. By the 1850s, the government saw a violent confrontation coming with the Dakota. Both government agencies and Indian advocacy groups of the period, such as the Indian Rights Association, sought to "civilize" rather than defeat the Dakota by changing them from nomadic hunters into settled farmers. It was also thought that assigning specific boundaries to each of the Indian nations would encourage the Plains tribes to give up warfare against each other and would lessen raiding on white farmers and settlers.

Superintendant of Indian Affairs D. D. Mitchell sent the following report after the conclusion of the Fort Laramie Treaty of 1851. It reveals the strategy that would be employed toward the Dakota for the next 40 years, throughout the second half of the 19th century.

> . . . The lessons of experience taught us during the Florida war, and which are now being taught us by the Indian wars in New Mexico, all admonish us of the necessity of avoiding Indian wars, if possible. Humanity calls loudly for some interposition on the part of the American government to save, if possible, some portion of these ill-fated tribes; and this, it is thought, can only be done by furnishing them with the means, and gradually turning their attention to agricultural pursuits. Without some aid from the government, it will be impossible for them to make an attempt even as graziers. Fifty years it was thought would be time sufficient to give the experiment a fair trial, and solve the great problem whether or not an Indian can be made a civilized man. The laying off of the country into geographical or rather national domains, I regard as a very important measure, inasmuch as it will take away a great cause of quarrel among themselves, and at the same time enable the government to ascertain who are the depredators, should depredations hereafter be committed. The accompanying map, upon which these national boundaries are clearly marked and defined, was made in the presence of the Indians, and fully approved and sanctioned by all . . .

by the treaty's Article 2, the Indians recognized " . . . the right of the United States Government to establish roads, military and other posts, within their respective territories."

In return, the government would protect the Indians from the emigrants and pay an annuity of $50,000 in "provisions, merchandise, domestic animals, and agricultural implements." According to the original agreement, payments were to be made for 50 years. But the U.S. Senate would change that figure to 10 years before ratifying the treaty. The president would have the option to renew the terms every five years—an option that would never be exercised.

The Lakota trusted that the Fort Laramie treaty would keep the whites out of their hunting grounds for good. But in the years to follow, the Lakota would have to keep fighting for their own land. In 1852, 22 prospectors were killed while searching for gold in the Black Hills. In 1854, a confrontation over an emigrant's wandering cow led to a battle near Fort Laramie. The fort's commander, Lieutenant Charles Grattan, marched into the village of Chief Conquering Bear, fired a volley into the Indians, and was then killed with his entire command. To retaliate, General W. S. Harney ordered a massacre of Lakota at Ash Hollow, near the Platte valley, and then led 1,200 soldiers through the heart of Lakota territory, from Fort Laramie to Fort Pierre on the Missouri River. The Indians offered no resistance to Harney's show of force.

Meanwhile, the westward migrations of the whites continued to shrink the buffalo herds and bring sickness and violence. To solve the problem, the Dakota Indians called a great council together in the summer of 1857 at the foot of Bear Butte near the Black Hills. It was decided that all the Dakota bands must stand together to resist any further white encroachment into their country. No more presents would be accepted and no more treaties would be signed. Any Dakota who signed agreements with the whites would be treated as an enemy; any who helped the whites in their search for gold in the Black Hills would be put to death.

The Dakota believed the great council at Bear Butte would protect their homeland. The U.S. government believed that the Fort Laramie treaty would bring peace to the Platte valley and to the northern Great Plains. But to the people of the United States, the northern Plains was still open frontier, to be fought for, claimed, settled, farmed, and civilized—treaties or no treaties. Kansas and eastern Colorado, where the invasion from the east had already advanced to the foothills of the Rocky Mountains, served as a warning of what was to come. In 1859, Commissioner A. B. Greenwood wrote:

> Since the discovery of gold in the vicinity of Pike's Peak, the emigration has immensely increased; the Indians have been driven from their local . . . hunting grounds, and the game so far killed off . . . , that it is now impossible for the Indians to obtain the necessary subsistence . . . we have substantially taken possession of the country and deprived them of their accustomed means of support.

In the same year, the Yankton Dakota signed a treaty selling their lands east of the Missouri River. In 1861, the United States organized the Dakota Territory, which stretched from the western border of Minnesota to the eastern ranges of the Rocky Mountains. To the south, a new telegraph line along the Platte River now allowed rapid communication between the east and west coasts. All around the Lakota lands, settlers were raising new frontier towns and establishing farms and livestock herds. The 1862 Homestead Act allowed them to claim 160 acres of free land ceded by the Indians in the newly organized territories.

While Lakota raids on the Platte valley continued, the fear of Indians drove many emigrants away from the Overland Trail and white settlers from the Nebraska plains. In 1862, an uprising among the Santee Dakota in Minnesota caused the deaths of more than 500 settlers. Although the Lakota were not involved, the massacres increased white suspicion and hostility toward all the Dakota bands.

Despite the fighting, the westward migration continued. In 1863, an explorer named John Bozeman blazed a trail from the Oregon Trail northward to Montana, where gold discoveries were bringing in a wave of prospectors. The trail led directly through the western hunting grounds of the Lakota. To protect the white

This illustration from *Harper's* depicts the Sioux Uprising of 1862. The event caused widespread fear and suspicion toward the Dakota tribes. *(From* Harper's New Monthly Magazine, *October 1875; the Minnesota Historical Society)*

prospectors and migrants, the U.S. Army raised a series of forts along the trail: Fort Reno, Fort Phil Kearny, and Fort C. F. Smith.

At the same time, Lakota, Cheyenne, and Arapaho warriors were raiding ranches, stagecoaches, trading posts, and forts along the Platte River and in the Powder River country along the Bozeman Trail. To bring some peace to the region, the government offered a new treaty to the Dakota tribes in 1865. The Indians were to respect the authority of the U.S. government. They were to cease raiding and allow the whites to pass peacefully through their territory. In exchange, the government would make annuity payments to help the Indians give up the buffalo hunt and take up farming. Government agencies would be built wherever a permanent farming community had been established. The agencies would supply merchandise and food; in addition, the government would place a blacksmith, a farmer, and a school teacher at the Indians' service to help the transition to a settled life.

In October 1865, leaders of the seven Lakota tribes signed the treaty. But it was rejected by the most important Lakota chiefs: Sitting Bull of the Hunkpapa, Spotted Tail of the Brulé, and Red Cloud of the Oglala. Red Cloud and an Oglala warrior named Crazy Horse, with Miniconjou, Brulé, and Oglala warriors, as well as Cheyenne and Arapaho, began a campaign against the forts in the Powder River country. The army did not have enough troops to stop the raiding parties and found itself unable to secure the Bozeman Trail.

In 1867, the government resolved to make peace with the Lakota, even at the price of closing the Bozeman Trail. Another treaty commission, under Superintendant N. G. Taylor, traveled to Fort Laramie to meet with the Lakota chiefs. This time, the negotiations were not entirely friendly. At the treaty council at Fort Laramie in April 1868, the Brulé chief Iron Shell declared "You have come into my country without my consent and spread your soldiers all over it. I have looked around for the cause of the trouble and I can not see that my young men were the cause of it . . . We want you to take away the forts from the country. That will leave room for the Indians to live in. If you succeed about the forts all the game will come back and we will have plenty to eat. If you want the Indian to live do that and we will have a chance to live." After hearing the treaty commission promise to remove the forts, these chiefs agreed to sign the treaty on April 29. A group of Oglala and Miniconjou chiefs signed the treaty in May; Santee, Yanktonai, and northern Lakota signed that summer.

But before he would sign any new treaty, Red Cloud demanded that the United States carry out its promise. The treaty commission agreed. In late 1868, with Red Cloud and his warriors watching, the army abandoned the forts and the Powder River country. With the army columns still in view, Red Cloud led his warriors into the forts, where they burned the buildings to the ground.

Red Cloud signed the second Fort Laramie treaty on November 26, 1868; the treaty was ratified by the Senate on February 24, 1869. The treaty surrendered the Powder River hunting grounds to the Lakota but also established the Great Sioux Reservation. The

United States drew new lines along the boundaries of what is now South Dakota west of the Missouri River. The seven Lakota groups would hold this land in common; it would be off limits to white settlement. Other lands belonging to the Lakota—the hunting grounds of the Powder River country and in Nebraska north of the North Platte River—became "unceded territory." The Lakota would be free to roam and hunt in these lands, but they could not settle there and must allow the United States to build roads and railroads through them.

For each of the groups an agency would be built. The agency would be a permanent U.S. outpost where rations would be distributed, annuities would be paid, and an agent would live with and watch over the Indians. Each agency would also have a physician, blacksmith, carpenter, miller, farmer, and engineer. A schoolhouse would be built for the education of Indian children.

Like the 1851 Fort Laramie treaty, the 1868 treaty meant to encourage permanent settlement by the Indians on their land. This time, the United States sought to apply the homestead laws to the Indians in the ongoing effort to "civilize" them. Indian families were allowed title to 320 acres of land within the reservation for their own use. Reservation land would gradually be privatized. The title to the land would confer U.S. citizenship on its holder, who also had the right to $100 worth of seeds and tools in the first year and $25 worth in the next three years.

No whites would be allowed to enter, cross, or settle in the Great Sioux Reservation or in the unceded territory without the permission of the Indians and of the government agents assigned to the reservation. In addition, by Article 12,

> No treaty for the cession of any portion or part of the reservation herein described . . . shall be of any validity or force unless executed and signed by at least three-fourths of all the adult male Indians, occupying . . . the same . . .

With settlement still sparse in eastern Dakota Territory, the authors of the treaty saw little possibility for conflict in the region.

But Sitting Bull and his followers had not signed the treaty, and it soon became clear to many whites that the Powder River region, where these "non-treaty" Indians roamed, was too valuable to leave as free and open hunting grounds for hostile Lakota. There was gold in the riverbeds and hills of this country, and white prospectors were determined to have access to it.

NOTES

p. vi   "The Sioux roamed . . ." Dr. Charles A. Eastman. *From the Deep Woods to Civilization: Chapters in the Autobiography of an Indian* (Lincoln: University of Nebraska Press, 1977), pp. 4–5.

pp. vii–viii   " . . . the Sioux possess . . ." Donald Jackson, ed. *Letters of the Lewis and Clark Expedition* (Urbana: University of Illinois Press, 1962), pp. 228–229.

p. viii   "It is admitted . . ." Don C. Clowser. *Dakota Indian Treaties: From Nomad to Reservation* (Deadwood, S.D.: Don C. Clowser, 1974), p. 10.

p. x   "The Ogillallah, the Brulé . . ." Francis Parkman, Jr. *The Oregon Trail*. Edited by E. N. Feltskog (Madison: University of Wisconsin Press, 1969), p. 117.

p. xi   "I . . . was much surprised . . ." Commissioner of Indian Affairs, *Annual Report 1851*.

p. xii   " . . . The lessons of experience . . ." *Report of the Commissioner of Indian Affairs*, 1851, p. 324.

p. xiv   "Since the discovery of gold . . ." Commissioner of Indian Affairs, *Annual Report 1859*.

p. xvi   "You have come into my country . . ." Clowser, p. 123.

p. xvii   "No treaty . . ." Peter Matthieson. *In the Spirit of Crazy Horse* (New York: Viking Press, 1980), p. 7.

1 THE GREAT SIOUX RESERVATION

A fter the Lakota chiefs signed the Treaty of 1868, the government built new agencies on or near the Great Sioux Reservation, which covered 90,000 square miles of dry plains, winding creek valleys, barren badlands, and the Black Hills. The Crow Creek and Lower Brulé agencies lay along the Missouri River south of Fort Pierre. Farther north, the Grand River and Cheyenne River agencies were built on the west bank of the river. Red Cloud and Spotted Tail agencies, named for the leading chiefs of the Oglala and Brulé, respectively, were in northern Nebraska, just off the reservation. The government expected the Lakota to settle near the agencies and give up their wandering life. They expected the Indians to complete the transition in about four years; according to the 1868 treaty, this was the period of guaranteed ration issues.

Meanwhile, the treaty system was changing. By a new law passed in 1871, Indian "treaties" became "agreements," which had to be passed by both houses of Congress, and signed by the president, rather than simply ratified by the Senate as were treaties with foreign powers. The Indians of the United States were no longer considered members of sovereign nations; instead, they were to be treated by congressional legislation. Management of

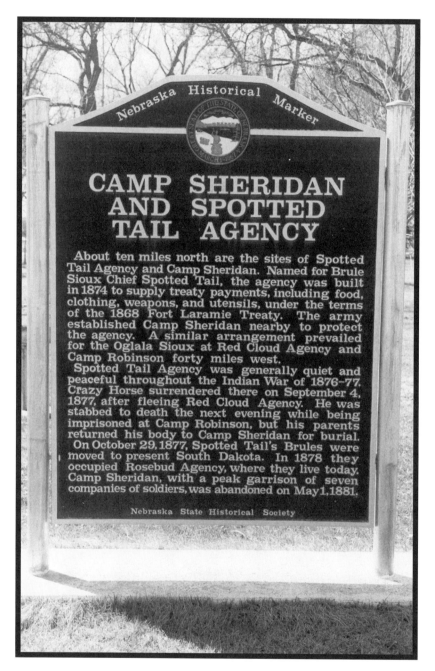

CAMP SHERIDAN AND SPOTTED TAIL AGENCY

About ten miles north are the sites of Spotted Tail Agency and Camp Sheridan. Named for Brule Sioux Chief Spotted Tail, the agency was built in 1874 to supply treaty payments, including food, clothing, weapons, and utensils, under the terms of the 1868 Fort Laramie Treaty. The army established Camp Sheridan nearby to protect the agency. A similar arrangement prevailed for the Oglala Sioux at Red Cloud Agency and Camp Robinson forty miles west.

Spotted Tail Agency was generally quiet and peaceful throughout the Indian War of 1876-77. Crazy Horse surrendered there on September 4, 1877, after fleeing Red Cloud Agency. He was stabbed to death the next evening while being imprisoned at Camp Robinson, but his parents returned his body to Camp Sheridan for burial.

On October 29, 1877, Spotted Tail's Brules were moved to present South Dakota. In 1878 they occupied Rosebud Agency, where they live today. Camp Sheridan, with a peak garrison of seven companies of soldiers, was abandoned on May 1, 1881.

Nebraska State Historical Society

A marker in the town of Hay Springs commemorates the Spotted Tail Agency. *(Photo by Tom Streissguth)* the Indian reservations was also changing. As part of a new "Peace Policy" devised by the Grant administration, the army officers who had served as government agents were now replaced by appointed civilians. Reservations came under the authority of the Indian Bureau, part of the Department of the Interior. A majority of lawmakers believed civilian management of the agencies would lessen conflict and help the Indians adopt farming.

The Treaty of 1868 did not end hostilities in the Powder River country, where an important group of Lakota leaders, including Sitting Bull and Crazy Horse, still roamed. These chiefs had not signed the treaty and would not abide by its provisions. They would not accept treaty presents or annuity goods; they would not demean themselves by planting and gathering crops. They continued to hunt the buffalo herds that survived west of the Black Hills; raid the Crow, the traditional enemy of the Dakota Indians; and make trouble for the United States. Throughout the early 1870s, these "non-treaty" Indians, as they were called by the whites, fought soldiers and civilians in the hunting grounds along the Yellowstone and Powder Rivers. Lakota also attacked survey crews who were measuring and marking land north of the reservation for the Northern Pacific Railroad. The bloodshed on the frontier caused growing hostility toward the Lakota among white farmers and townspeople living near the Great Sioux Reservation. By the mid-1870s, the promises of peace held out by the Treaty of 1868 had been forgotten on both sides.

The conflict soon came to the Black Hills. The Black Hills lay within the Great Sioux Reservation, and the Lakota had resolved to let no whites enter or pass through them. But there was one important element that was now prompting many whites to over-look treaty articles and ignore reservation boundaries. Miners had found gold in Montana; they had struck it rich in the streams of California and the deserts of Nevada. There might also be gold in the Black Hills, one of the last unexplored regions of the western United States.

Custer (center) and his guides pose with their quarry during the Black Hills expedition of 1874. *(Photo: Illingworth. From the Minnesota Historical Society)*

As the government saw things, the continuing Teton raids in the Powder River country and along the Platte River in Nebraska gave the army an excuse to stage a march into the Black Hills. At Chicago, headquarters of the army's Division of the Missouri, Lieutenant General Phillip H. Sheridan wrote the following to General W. T. Sherman, U.S. Army commander in Washington: "I would like to start Colonel Custer with a column of cavalry out, about the 15th of June, to examine the Black Hills country and the north fork of the Cheyenne, known on the map as the Belle

Fourche. This country is entirely unknown, and a knowledge of it might be of great value in case of Indian troubles."

Sheridan believed the army should try to prevent the non-treaty Lakota from using the Black Hills as a refuge and as a staging ground for their raids and war parties. He planned to survey the area and, when the time was right, build an army outpost in the Black Hills. But the 1874 expedition, which was soon approved by the War Department, quickly turned into much more than a military reconnaissance. Colonel Frederick D. Grant, the son of President Ulysses S. Grant, would join George Armstrong Custer, the expedition's commander. The U.S. government also hired miners and geologists to accompany the troops. There would be an official show of force to intimidate the Lakota; there would also be a survey for gold.

On July 2, 1874, the Black Hills expedition set out from Fort Abraham Lincoln with about 700 soldiers of the Seventh Cavalry and about 300 civilians. The long column trundled over the Dakota prairies alongside more than 100 supply wagons and a large herd of beef cattle. Despite the well-publicized dangers described by newspaper and magazine reports, the expedition encountered no hostile Indians and turned into a picnic for the troops. According to one Seventh Cavalry soldier, Private Charles Windolph,

> We'd make great campfires and almost every evening
> there'd be a band concert . . . We had a mighty fine
> band, and on the nights when the moon was out and the
> stars cracking in the sky, and the air was crisp and cool,
> it was something to stretch out before a big open log fire
> and listen to the music. Soldiering wasn't half bad those
> times . . . .

In late July, from his field headquarters near Harney Peak in the Black Hills, Custer sent a dispatch describing what he'd seen. He praised the soil and grazing; he described the mild climate, the abundant timber, the cool streams, and the delicious wild berries. He also observed:

> . . . gold has been found at several places, and it is the be-
> lief of those who are giving their attention to this subject
> that it will be found in paying quantities.

Custer sent a dispatch rider, Lonesome Charley Reynolds, to Fort Laramie with the reports. From Laramie the news was telegraphed to army headquarters and newspaper offices. In August, Custer returned to Fort Lincoln. The Black Hills gold rush had begun.

Word of the discoveries spread quickly via newspaper and magazine reports. That fall, a civilian expedition entered the Black Hills and built a stockade along French Creek, the site of the first gold strike. In the United States, it was a time of economic depression and high unemployment, and the prospect of staking gold claims in this "empty" country brought thousands of fortune seekers to the hills. Setting off from small towns on the Missouri River, they flooded westward across the Dakota reservation; many were camping in the Black Hills by the summer of 1875. Rowdy frontier towns such as Deadwood and Custer grew rapidly in the midst of the sacred *Paha Sapa* of the Great Sioux Reservation.

A half-hearted attempt by the military to protect the Black Hills from white encroachment failed completely. In his report for the year 1875, the commissioner of Indian Affairs wrote:

> However unwilling we may be to confess it, the experi-
> ence of the past summer proves either the inefficiency of
> the large military force under the command of such offi-
> cers as Generals Sheridan, Terry, and Crook, or the utter
> impracticability of keeping Americans out of a country
> where gold is known to exist by any fear of orders or of
> United States cavalry, or by any consideration of the
> rights of others.

While miners and soldiers broke the government's 1868 treaty, many reservation Indians were moving westward to join the non-treaty chiefs in the Powder River country. Arapaho, Cheyenne, and even Santee Dakota from east of the Missouri River camped with the Lakota, spelling trouble for the small cavalry

GENERAL CROOK'S PROCLAMATION TO MINERS TRESPASSING IN THE BLACK HILLS

Although the U.S. government was legally obliged, by treaty, to remove trespassers from the Black Hills, the effort was half-hearted and entirely unsuccessful. Gold fever had seized the whites, and the Black Hills region was quickly inundated with prospectors and speculators. In his book *On the Border with Crook*, John G. Bourke gave a firsthand account of the Black Hills gold rush:

> Cheyenne was then wild with excitement concerning the Indian war, which all the old frontiersmen felt was approaching, and the settlement of the Black Hills, in which gold in unheard-of sums was alleged to be hidden. No story was too wild, too absurd, to be swallowed with eagerness and published as a fact in the papers of the town. Along the streets were camped long trains of wagons loading for the Black Hills; every store advertised a supply of goods suited to the Black Hills trade; the hotels were crowded with men on their way to the new El Dorado; even the stage-drivers, boot-blacks, and bell-boys could talk nothing but Black Hills—Black Hills.

Recognizing that the army could not stop the tide of prospectors, Brigadier General George Crook, commander of the Department of the Platte, tried friendly persuasion while building his own camp near Harney Peak, the highest point in the Black Hills. In his proclamation formally expelling the Black Hills miners in the summer of 1875, Crook held out the promise of future white ownership of the Black Hills, advising those trespassers he was evicting to keep a legal record of their still-illegal claims: " . . . It is suggested that the miners now in the hills . . . hold a meeting and take such steps as may seem best to them by organization and the drafting of proper resolutions to secure to each, when the country shall have been opened, the benefit of his discovery and the labor he has already expended. George Crook, Brig. Gen. U.S.A. Comd. Dept of the Platte."

units attempting to corral the growing force of Indians. Skirmishes took place between the cavalry and the "hostiles," and western Dakota Territory again became dangerous country for the whites. Wrote Elizabeth Custer, the wife of George Armstrong Custer,

> A large number of Indians who fought us were fresh from their reservations on the Missouri River. Many of the warriors . . . were dressed in complete suits of clothes issued at the agencies. We found provisions, such as coffee, in their abandoned camps, and cooking and other domestic utensils, such as only reservation Indians are supplied with.

Again unable to stop white trespass on reservation land, the government invited Red Cloud, Spotted Tail, and other "progressive" chiefs to Washington to negotiate the outright sale of the

This sign in the western Nebraska plains recounts the many battles and historic events that took place in the region. *(Photo by Tom Streissguth)*

Black Hills. At one point, the government negotiators asked the Lakota to give up their reservation altogether and move to Indian Territory (modern-day Oklahoma). The government also demanded that the Lakota give up their right to hunt in unceded lands south of the Great Sioux Reservation. The two chiefs did agree to sell these rights for $25,000 but refused to move away from their homeland or to sell the Black Hills for any sum.

Negotiations for outright purchase having failed, a commission headed by Senator William Allison set out in September 1875 to arrange a lease of the Black Hills for the white miners. Red Cloud, Spotted Tail, and several thousand reservation Indians met the commissioners at a spot near Red Cloud Agency, in northwestern Nebraska. A huge band of hostile Lakota also arrived, determined to prevent any new treaty. The warriors refused to meet the commissioners and, at one point, swept down into the camp and threatened death to the whites and to any chief who would sell the Black Hills.

Nevertheless, the chiefs at the treaty council set their price: $7 million. Red Cloud declared to the commission:

> These Hills out here to the northwest we look upon as
> the head chief of the land. My intention was that my
> children depend on these for the future. I think that the
> Black Hills are worth more than all the wild beasts and
> all the tame beasts in the possession of the white people.
> I know it well, and you can see it plain enough, that God
> Almighty placed these Hills here for my wealth, but
> now you want to take them from me and make me poor,
> so I ask so much that I won't be poor.

The commissioners then made their own offer: to rent the Black Hills for mining, farming, and settlement for $400,000 per year; or to buy them outright for $6 million, to be paid in 15 annual installments. The negotiations broke off without an agreement.

In the eyes of the government, the hostile Indians roaming the Powder River country posed the most serious obstacle to the purchase of the Black Hills. In December 1875, therefore, the United States simply ordered the Lakota to abandon all unceded territory, including the Powder River country, and settle permanently on the reservation by January 31, 1876. Sitting Bull, Crazy Horse, and other Lakota chiefs did not—and could not—comply. The weather was too cold for travel; even had they been able to make the journey, the agencies did not have enough food for them.

When the January deadline passed, the War Department began planning a campaign against Crazy Horse and Sitting Bull. Generals Custer, Terry, and Crook marched their soldiers into the hunting grounds along the Powder River.

That spring, Sitting Bull invited the Lakota to leave the Great Sioux Reservation and join his followers in the unceded territory. "We want no white men here," Sitting Bull declared. "The Black Hills belong to me. If the whites try to take them, I will fight." Thousands responded, gathering in huge camps along Rosebud Creek, a small tributary of the Yellowstone River. The generals were confident that their forces were strong enough to overwhelm these Indians. But on June 17, Crazy Horse and a thousand warriors stopped General Crook's column in a narrow canyon along the Rosebud. A week later, on June 25, several thousand Lakota and Cheyenne warriors defeated General Custer's Seventh Cavalry at the Little Bighorn River, east of the Rosebud. Custer's entire command of 252 men, as well as five civilians and three scouts, were killed in the battle, the worst defeat suffered by the army in its entire history of Indian fighting.

After Custer's defeat, General Crook marched his troops from the Yellowstone River south to the Black Hills, determined to punish the hostile Lakota and chase them onto the reservation. Crook's force surprised and attacked a Lakota village at Slim Buttes, killing the chief American Horse. The Cheyenne allies of the Lakota scattered away from the soldiers; many Lakota took refuge near the reservation agencies. In the fall, General Terry was pursuing Sitting Bull across northern Montana, while General Miles raided Lakota and Cheyenne camps along the Powder River and prepared for a winter campaign in the unceded territory. Crook surrounded Red Cloud's camp, confiscating guns and turning the village's entire pony herd over to a band of Pawnee.

EYEWITNESS AT THE LITTLE BIGHORN

In 1931, 55 years after the Battle of the Greasy Grass (Little Bighorn), She Walks with Her Shawl, a Hunkpapa woman, described what she had seen at the fight to historian Walter S. Campbell:

> . . . I was several miles from the Hunkpapa camp when I saw a cloud of dust rise beyond a ridge of bluffs in the east . . . We girls looked towards the camp and saw a warrior ride swiftly, shouting that the soldiers were only a few miles away and that the women and children including old men should run for the hills in an opposite direction.
>
> . . . We crossed the Greasy Grass below a beaver dam (the water is not so deep there) and came upon many horses. One soldier was holding the reins of eight or ten horses. An Indian waved his blanket and scared all the horses. They got away from the men (troopers). On the ridge just north of us I saw blue-clad men running up a ravine, firing as they ran.
>
> The dust created from the stampeding horses and powder smoke made everything dark and black. Flashes from carbines could be seen. The valley was dense with powder smoke. I never heard such whooping and shouting. "There was never a better day to die," shouted Red Horse . . . .
>
> Long Hair's troopers were trapped in an enclosure. There were Indians everywhere. The Cheyennes attacked the soldiers from the north and Crow King from the South. The Sioux Indians encircled the troopers. Not one got away! The Sioux used tomahawks. It was not a massacre, but [a] hotly contested battle between two armed forces. Very few soldiers were mutilated, as oft has been said by the whites. Not a single soldier was burned at the stake. Sioux Indians do not torture their victims.

With their horses and winter supplies seized, the bands of non-treaty Lakota began to surrender.

In the meantime, by the Indian Appropriation Act of 1876, the U.S. Congress had resolved to end all money for rations and annuities to the Lakota unless an agreement could be made for the cession of the Powder River hunting grounds and the Black Hills. To lawmakers in Washington, the unstoppable settlement of the Black Hills by white prospectors, and the death of Custer and his

A stone pillar and a historical marker indicate the site of the Red Cloud Agency, near Fort Robinson in northwestern Nebraska. At this spot the U.S. government laid down its terms for surrender of the Black Hills. *(Photos by Tom Streissguth)*

soldiers, justified the army's winter campaign and a new treaty. In Congress, a delegate from Dakota Territory named Jefferson Kidder declared:

> The Black Hills have become occupied by a large popula-
> tion of the bold and hardy yeomanry of our country . . .
> But the Indians are continually murdering innocent
> men, women, and children. Remove this dusky cloud
> from a portion of the reservation . . . and it will stop the
> shedding of innocent blood.

The government sent another treaty commission to Red Cloud Agency to work out the details. This time, the United States simply set down the terms, which by a popular slogan were simply "sell or starve." Not strong enough to defeat or stalemate the army, and no longer able to survive by hunting, Red Cloud, Spotted Tail, and other Lakota leaders signed the agreement in October 1876. The Lakota gave up the Powder River hunting grounds, the Black Hills, and the portion of the Great Sioux Reservation lying between 103 degrees and 104 degrees longitude. They also agreed to allow the construction of three roads across the reservation from the Missouri River to the Black Hills. In return, the United States agreed to provide rations to all Lakota living on the reservation until the Indians became self-supporting farmers. Although nearly 400 Indians marked the agreement, the commission did not obtain the signatures of three-fourths of all Lakota adult men, as was required by the Treaty of 1868. This detail didn't concern the U.S. Congress, which ratified the new agreement on February 28, 1877.

Scattered and half-starved, the non-treaty Lakota leaders began giving up the fight and moving to the government agencies. Red Cloud and his Oglala followers settled permanently at Red Cloud Agency, which lay along the White River in northwestern Nebraska. Spotted Tail's Brulé moved to Spotted Tail Agency, to the east. In the fall of 1877 these two agencies would be moved north, just over the border of the Great Sioux Reservation. The Oglala were settled at Pine Ridge Agency; the Brulé at Rosebud. Farther north, the government assigned the Miniconjou tribe to the

A pyramidal stone monument marks the site of the death of Crazy Horse at Fort Robinson. *(Photo by Tom Streissguth)*

Cheyenne River Agency; the Grand River Agency was to be the home of the Hunkpapa.

Pursued by General Terry, Sitting Bull and 2,500 members of his Hunkpapa tribe fled to Canada in 1877. They were joined by some of the followers of Crazy Horse, who was killed that May after surrendering at Fort Robinson. There were no reservations marked or treaties signed in Canada; instead of campaigning against Sitting Bull, the Royal Northwest Mounted Police left the Lakota camps in peace. When General Terry came north to persuade Sitting Bull to return to the reservation, the chief sternly refused. "Go back home where you came from," Sitting Bull replied. "This country is my country now, and I intend to stay here and raise people to fill it . . . The country that belonged to us, you ran me out of it. I have come here, and here I intend to stay. I want you to go back, and take it easy going back."

But with the buffalo disappearing from the northern ranges, Sitting Bull's band went hungry and found life no better in the

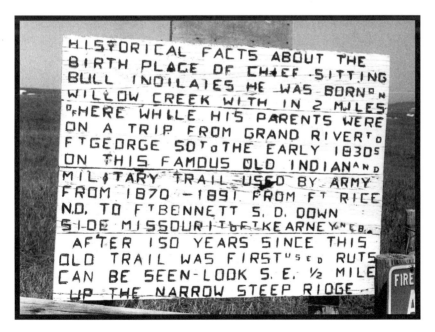

A weathered sign marks the birthplace of Sitting Bull on the plains west of the Missouri River. *(Photo by Tom Streissguth)*

"Great Mother's" (Queen Victoria's) country than it had been in the unceded territory along the Powder River. Promised a pardon if he would lead his people back to the reservation, Sitting Bull finally surrendered at Fort Buford, Montana, on July 19, 1881. After spending two years in a jail at Fort Randall, on the Missouri River, he moved to a settlement along the Grand River, southwest of the Standing Rock Agency. There he stayed, the most prominent leader of the non-treaty Lakota, to keep up resistance to the demands and expectations of the whites and of his rivals among the progressive Lakota leaders.

NOTES

pp. 4–5 "I would like to start Colonel Custer . . ." Clowser, p. 161.

p. 5 "We'd make great campfires . . ." James Welch. *Killing Custer: The Battle of the Little Bighorn and the Fate of the Plains Indians* (New York: W.W. Norton, 1994), p. 82.

p. 6 ". . . gold has been found . . ." Clowser, pp. 169–170.

p. 6 "However unwilling we may be . . ." Commissioner of Indian Affairs, *Annual Report 1874.*

p. 7 "Cheyenne was then . . ." John G. Bourke. *On the Border with Crook* (New York: Charles Scribner's Sons, 1891), pp. 247–248.

p. 7 "It is suggested . . ." Clowser, p. 179.

p. 8 "A large number of Indians . . ." Elizabeth Custer. *Boots and Saddles* (New York: Harper and Brothers, 1885), p. 289, quoted in Charles L. Green. *The Indian Reservation System of the Dakotas, South Dakota Historical Collections* 14 (Pierre: South Dakota Historical Society, 1928), p. 373.

p. 9 "These Hills out here to the northwest . . ." Edward Lazarus. *Black Hills, White Justice: The Sioux Nation Versus the United States* (New York: HarperCollins, 1991), p. 82.

p. 10 "We want no white men . . ." Matthieson, p. 10.

p. 11 ". . . I was several miles from . . ." Jerome A. Greene, ed. *Lakota and Cheyenne: Indian Views of the Great Sioux War 1876–1877* (Norman: University of Oklahoma Press, 1994), p. 45.

p. 13   "The Black Hills have become occupied . . ." Rex Alan Smith. *Moon of Popping Trees: The Tragedy of Wounded Knee and the End of the Indian Wars* (Lincoln: University of Nebraska Press, 1975), p. 58.

p. 15   "Go back home . . ." Stanley Vestal [Walter S. Campbell]. *Warpath and Council Fire: The Plains Indians' Struggle for Survival in War and in Diplomacy 1851–1891* (New York: Random House, 1948), p. 285.

2 LEAVING THE OLD WAYS BEHIND

The Treaty of 1868 and the Agreement of 1876 demanded more than land from the Lakota. The United States also asked the Lakota to adopt, in the course of a few years, an entirely different way of life—to make a transformation that had occurred over thousands of years for the European ancestors of the whites. Instead of nomads, the Indians must become farmers. Instead of hunting the buffalo for their food, clothing, and shelter, and living in communal villages, they must now settle permanently on separate tracts of land, break the soil, and raise crops in the extreme climate of western Dakota. The band camps would disappear; the Lakota would be scattered across their reservation just as white settlers were spread around the new territories and states that now surrounded the Indians on the Great Plains. The Indians must give up their traditional religion and dances, send their children to government schools, and stop making war on rival tribes.

According to Article 5 of the Agreement of 1876, "In consideration of the foregoing cession of territory and rights . . . the United States does agree to provide all necessary aid to assist the said Indians in the work of civilization." Until they adapted to the white man's life, the Lakota would have the right to draw regular

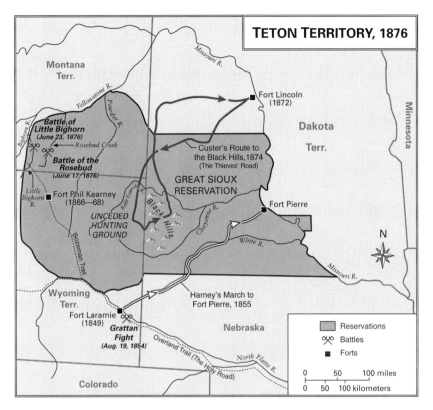

TETON TERRITORY, 1876

Montana Terr.

Missouri R.

Yellowstone R.

Powder R.

Bighorn R.

Battle of Little Bighorn (June 23, 1876)

Rosebud Creek

Battle of the Rosebud (June 17, 1876)

Little Bighorn R.

Fort Phil Kearney (1866—68)

UNCEDED HUNTING GROUND

Bozeman Trail

Belle Fourche R.

Black Hills

Fort Lincoln (1872)

Dakota Terr.

Custer's Route to the Black Hills, 1874 (The Thieves' Road)

GREAT SIOUX RESERVATION

Cheyenne R.

Fort Pierre

White R.

Missouri R.

Minnesota

N

Wyoming Terr.

Fort Laramie (1849)

Grattan Fight (Aug. 19, 1854)

Harney's March to Fort Pierre, 1855

Nebraska

Overland Trail (The Holy Road)

North Platte R.

Colorado

Reservations
Battles
Forts

0	50	100 miles
0	50	100 kilometers

The Treaty of 1868 created the Great Sioux Reservation as well as a region of unceded hunting grounds lying west of the Black Hills.

rations of food. In detail, that meant the government would issue just enough beef or bacon, flour, corn, coffee, sugar, and beans for them to survive. However, " . . . whenever schools shall have been provided by the Government for said Indians, no rations shall be issued for children between the ages of six and fourteen years (the sick and infirm excepted) unless such children shall regularly attend school."

They would draw regular payments for the surrender of their lands to the whites. The government would help them learn farming and build homes and schools. Also, by Article 5, " . . . the Government will aid such Indians as far as possible in finding a market for their surplus productions, and in finding employment, and will purchase such surplus, as far as may be required, for supplying food to those Indians . . . who are unable to sustain themselves." When the Lakota were finally able to support themselves entirely through crop- and livestock-raising, the rations would stop. In 1879, the government issued 3,000 head of cattle to the Lakota agencies to provide a start to a reservation livestock herd.

Some of the Lakota leaders accepted the government's terms and settled down to the new life, plowing and planting small acreages under the direction of the white agency farmers. In this group was Young Man Afraid of His Horses, a "progressive" member of the Oglala tribe. By 1885, the Lakota of the Cheyenne River Agency were cultivating 1,621 acres. Acreage plowed by the Brulé at Rosebud reached 4,000 acres in 1886.

Many others were not ready to surrender their traditions. "Father, the Great Spirit did not make us to work," declared Red Cloud to the Pine Ridge agent. "He made us to hunt and fish. He gave us the plains and the hills and covered them with the buffalo . . . The white man can work if he wants to, but the Great Spirit did not make us to work." The promise of ongoing rations also gave many Lakota a strong incentive to stay out of the fields and remain unharnessed to any plow. Agent James McLaughlin of the Standing Rock Agency reported that the Lakota "do not wish to cultivate large fields or raise surplus crops . . . they might be dropped from the ration rolls and obliged to support themselves thereafter."

To assist the drive toward civilization, McLaughlin and the other agents did their best to undermine the authority of the nonprogressive Lakota chiefs. In 1880, Agent McGillycuddy at Pine Ridge began distributing rations to each family head, instead of to the Oglala chiefs. McGillycuddy also recruited a volunteer police force under the leadership of a progressive Oglala named George Sword. A permanent council was established, with the progressive leader Young Man Afraid of His Horses serving as president. The "nonprogressive" Indians found themselves cut off from the favor of the agents, from employment, and sometimes from their due rations. Meanwhile, as Lakota moved out to farm their homesteads, the camps near the agencies slowly dwindled, shrinking the power of the traditional camp leaders.

The agents, missions, and schools on the reservation were working for a common goal—turning the Lakota into god-fearing and English-speaking frontier settlers. They were wholeheartedly supported in this policy by the Congress, the Department of the Interior, the Indian Rights Association, and other lobbying groups working in eastern cities on the Indians' behalf. To support the reservation agents, the commissioner of Indian Affairs passed several important decrees in April 1883. The Lakota could no longer hold traditional dances, including the Sun Dance, or practice polygamy. The work of medicine men was outlawed, as were traditional marriage customs. At each agency, special courts were set up to try these offenses; progressive Indians sat on the court as judges.

As intended, measures such as these were effectively destroying traditional Lakota culture; unintentionally, they were turning the Lakota people dependent and resentful. In 1883 occurred the last Sun Dance and the last buffalo hunt on the northern Great Plains. According to Elaine Goodale Eastman—educator of Indians and later wife of Santee Dakota physician Charles A. Eastman —the hunt

> marked . . . the end of their independence as a nation. There remained a confused, depressed and humiliated dark folk, clad in a bizarre mixture of coarse jeans, gay calico, and shoddy blankets, subsisting literally from hand to mouth upon a monthly or fortnightly dole of beef, pork, flour, and coffee.

Together, the agents, the progressive chiefs, and the cavalry soldiers who occupied a ring of forts near the reservation made a strong case for acceptance of the government's terms. But there was nothing the progressive faction could do to change the harsh terms set down by the Dakota climate. Drought, storms, hail, and insects ravaged the meager crops; long and cold winters killed many of the cattle issued to the Lakota for establishing permanent

AT SCHOOL ON THE
PINE RIDGE AGENCY

The treaties made by the U.S. government with the Lakota provided for the establishment of public schools on the reservation. The government required Indian parents to send

Lakota students follow a music lesson at the Oahe Mission school. *(From the Minnesota Historical Society)*

herds. White settlers as well as Indians found themselves unable to make a living from the soil.

General Nelson Miles, U.S. Army commander of the Division of the Missouri, wrote:

> settlers have been most unfortunate, and their losses have been severe and universal . . . They have struggled on from year to year; occasionally they would raise good crops, which they were compelled to sell at low prices, while in the season of drought their labor was almost en-

children to these schools to learn English and the arts and crafts necessary for survival in the new civilization.

The schoolteachers were determined to remove the influences of the old, nomadic life and make Indian children adopt white ways. This went as far as changing their dress, hair, and especially their names, to help them forget their traditions. As one teacher at Pine Ridge Agency described it:

> The teachers had prepared a list of simple, easily-pronounced names, and they were assigned to the newcomers along with the names of their family . . . but translated into atrocious English. For example: Dan Swift Hawk, John Two Dogs, Robert Dogs, Robert Iron Horse, Eliza Buffalo Head, Elizabeth Kills Enemy. They could then be enrolled and placed in classes.
>
> The Head Matron then employed in the school placed great importance upon the girls braiding their hair in one braid. She thought changing the mode of hair dress broke one more thread that bound the Indian girl to her camplife, so she made it an offence against a rule of the school for a girl to comb her hair camp style, which was to part it down the middle of the head from the forehead to the nape of the neck and braid each half tightly from behind the ears, framing the face as she thought most becomingly when it lay upon her chest. . . .
>
> Another offence was for the girls to pluck out their eyebrows. This gave a decided Mona Lisa expression to their faces that they thought also added much to their good looks. As a result of this over-emphasis on the unimportant, when something at the school had really gone wrong, and the girls felt a spirit of rebellion within them, they would manage not to be seen doing it, nor heard protesting, but would suddenly appear with their hair in two braids and their eyebrows plucked.

tirely lost. So serious have been their misfortunes that thousands have left the country within the last few years, passing over the mountains to the Pacific slope or returning to the east of the Missouri or the Mississippi.

The Lakota, of course, could not move off their reservation or homestead somewhere else. Some found regular employment on white ranches or as freight drivers, who transported goods to the agencies. The rest continued to depend on rations to support their families.

At the same time, the tide of white migration to the Black Hills was rising. By 1882, lawmakers in Washington had decided that the Great Sioux Reservation was blocking necessary transportation routes between the Missouri River and the Black Hills. Although the 1876 agreement had called for the construction of three roads, there was still only a single wagon road, and no railroad lines, running from Fort Pierre on the Missouri to the Deadwood Trail in the Black Hills. To reach the Black Hills, most whites had to travel a long, wearying route around the reservation on the Fremont, Elkhorn, and Missouri Valley Railroad, which linked the scattered frontier cities of northern Nebraska.

Pressure to claim more of the Great Sioux Reservation was rising. On March 11, 1882, a notice in the *Black Hills Daily Times* announced the following:

> There will be a mass meeting of the citizens of Lawrence, Pennington and Custer Counties in the courthouse at Deadwood, Wednesday, March 14, 1882, for the purpose of taking such steps as may be deemed advisable to secure and utilize the 45,000 square miles of grazing land in SW Dakota known as the Great Sioux Reservation, unequalled in America for its nutritious grasses, sufficient to sustain one million head of stock. The benefits to be derived from this must be obvious to all . . .

That year, Richard F. Pettigrew, a Congressional delegate from Dakota Territory, wrote a bill authorizing another treaty commission to negotiate with the Lakota. Under Newton Edmunds, a former territorial governor, the commission arrived at each of the agencies to ask for a new agreement that would surrender a wide right-of-way through the middle of the reservation. In 1883, the commission returned to Washington with the marks of 384 Lakota leaders—not three-quarters of the adult male population and thus not enough by the terms of the Treaty of 1868. The commission returned to Dakota but failed to persuade enough of the Lakota to sign. This time, the government recognized the failure of the commission to fulfill its legal requirement, and the proposed agreement died.

In Washington, meanwhile, citizens' groups lobbying for the Indians pressed for new legislation that would improve the situation on the western reservations. The cornerstone of this policy was a new Indian land-ownership law modeled on the 1862 Homestead Act. Reservation lands would be distributed as allotments to the heads of Indian households; those who claimed allotments would become U.S. citizens. By the General Allotment Act of 1887, known as the Dawes Act after its author, Senator Henry L. Dawes, reservation land in the United States that had not already been made available through the allotment system would now be offered to Indian families. The head of each family would be granted a title to 160 acres and then citizenship. The government would hold the official patents (deeds) for the land to prevent the Indians from selling the allotments or from being swindled out of them by land speculators. When all the Indians of a reservation had claimed their acreages, the remaining "surplus" land would be sold off to white homesteaders. The payments made to the government for these surplus lands would be used for Indian education and employment programs.

The Dawes Act was extended to the Lakota reservation by the Sioux Act of 1888. But the Sioux Act allowed the government to sell the surplus land *first*. The Great Sioux Reservation would become six much smaller reservations, to be marked off around the six agencies: Pine Ridge, Rosebud, Cheyenne River, Standing Rock, Crow Creek, and Lower Brulé. The government would buy the ceded land from the Lakota at the price of 50 cents an acre but would pay out the money only as it was collected from white homesteaders. Each Lakota family that claimed its own homestead would be provided with seeds, tools, a pair of oxen, a pair of cows, and $20 in cash.

Another commission was appointed the task of getting the necessary signatures to validate the Sioux Act of 1888. The commission was led by Captain Richard Pratt, the founder and head of the Carlisle Indian School in Pennsylvania. The new agreement was supported by many of Pratt's own Carlisle students, who had left their reservations to learn the English language and white ways. But Pratt failed to persuade most of the Lakota chiefs to put their marks to the treaty. He returned to Washington recommending that the treaty be put into effect without the necessary signatures.

In December 1888, Congressman Oscar S. Gifford drafted a bill to open reservation lands on new terms. By this law, Lakota families would have the right to claim 320 acres, and they would be paid $50 to improve their homesteads. Instead of 50 cents an acre for the "surplus" land, the tribes would be paid on a sliding scale, depending on when the land was homesteaded by white farmers. During the first three years, the price would be $1.25 per acre; the next two years it would be 75 cents an acre; and after five years 50 cents an acre. The proposed terms were included in the Sioux Act passed by Congress and signed on March 2, 1889 by President Benjamin Harrison.

By the Indian Appropriation Act of 1889, a new commission was appointed under Major General George Crook to bring the Sioux Act to the reservation. Having fought in the Powder River campaigns, Crook was well known to the Lakota leaders. He brought many years of experience to the negotiations and succeeded where Pratt had failed through patience, promises, and a strategy of dividing the Lakota into rival parties. "Last year when you refused to accept the bill, Congress came very near opening the reservation anyway," Crook told the Lakota. "It is certain that you will never get any better terms than are offered in this bill . . . and it strikes me that instead of your complaining of the past, you had better provide for the future." By this time, the government's pledges meant nothing to the nonprogressive faction, who believed the United States would simply take the land, end the rations, and let the Lakota fend for themselves. Once again, the Lakota were divided into bitterly hostile camps over the government's proposed agreement. But Crook's persuasive speeches in the treaty councils, and his promises that the government would not cut their rations, prompted several Lakota leaders to come forward and sign. Eventually, 4,463 out of 5,678 eligible Lakota men signed the Agreement of 1889—more than three-quarters.

In the meantime, the U.S. government was further undermining any remaining trust of the Lakota in its written agreements. In an effort to determine the precise numbers of Lakota who were drawing rations, the government had sent a census taker, A. C. Lea, out to Dakota Territory. Lea's census, which took two years to complete, found fewer Indians than had previously been claimed. The administration reasoned that the Indians were cheating the government, giving Congress an excuse to cut the annual appropriation for annuity goods and rations. By the Indian Appropriation Act—the same that had appointed the Crook Commission—Congress reduced the appropriation for rations on the Sioux reservation from $1 million to $900,000 a year. A short time after the Crook Commission departed, the reservation agents had to reduce rations. At Pine Ridge, agent Hugh Gallagher cut the beef ration by one million pounds a year.

To make the Agreement of 1889 more attractive, Crook had made several promises to the Lakota. The ban on ceremonial dancing would be lifted; Indians at Cheyenne River and Standing Rock would be paid for horses lost during the 1876 fighting; a fund for Indian education would be established. In December 1889, the Crook Commission brought a delegation of Lakota leaders to Washington to discuss these terms with the president and listen to an explanation of the ration cut. Crook and the other commissioners sought to conclude an agreement without deception or bitterness; the Harrison administration simply sought to conclude the agreement. The Lakota returned to their homes hopeful that Crook's promises would be fulfilled.

Harrison and the Republican party's victory in the presidential election of 1888 had brought important changes. A new political party in office meant new officers in the Indian Bureau and new agents on the reservations. General Thomas J. Morgan was appointed as the new commissioner of Indian Affairs. To curry favor with the voters of Dakota Territory, who favored the Republican party, the new administration supported a bill that would divide

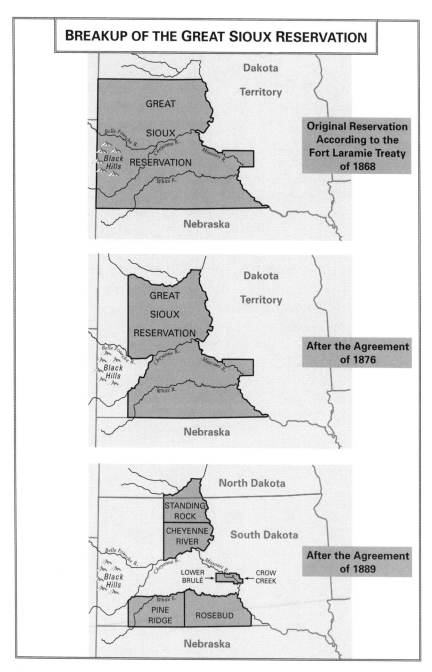

BREAKUP OF THE GREAT SIOUX RESERVATION

Original Reservation According to the Fort Laramie Treaty of 1868

After the Agreement of 1876

After the Agreement of 1889

The pressure of white settlement prompted the U.S. government, with the aid of its military, to force the gradual breakup of the Great Sioux Reservation established in 1868. By 1890, when the last agreement was signed and ratified, the reservation had been split up into six small territories.

the territory and grant statehood to North and South Dakota. A constitutional convention had been held in Sioux Falls, and the new state constitution had been ratified on July 4, 1889. Pierre was chosen as the state capital of South Dakota. That fall, voters elected the state's first two senators, Gideon C. Moody and Richard F. Pettigrew. President Harrison officially proclaimed statehood for South Dakota on November 2, 1889.

Harrison kept his promise to the Dakota Republicans who had supported him in the presidential election. But the government forgot the promises it had made to the Lakota for the sake of passing the agreement of 1889. In this action it was wholeheartedly supported by white voters and editorialists. "The Sioux Reservation contains over 22,000,000 acres," ran an editorial in the Sioux City *Journal*.

> That's one thousand acres for every Indian man, woman, and child. With the exception of about 20,000 acres adjacent to the agencies, this land is put to no use whatsoever by the Indians. The Indians now are almost entirely a helpless charge upon the government. Aside from holding a farm out for every one of them, male and female, the rest ought to go on the market that the development and civilization of the West may not be left to follow the slow movements of the development and civilization of the Indians. What the Indians will not do the white people ought to be permitted to do.

On February 10, 1890, President Benjamin Harrison announced that three-quarters of the Lakota had accepted the agreement. Lands ceded by the Teton bands would be opened immediately for settlement. In the meantime, there had been no allotments made to Indians living in ceded territory, and the cut in rations remained in force. The Lakota had been deceived again.

NOTES

p. 20   "Father, the Great Spirit . . ." Smith, p. 60.

p. 21   "marked . . . the end of their independence . . ." Elaine Goodale Eastman. "The Ghost Dance War and Wounded Knee Massacre of 1890–91," *Nebraska History,* 26 (Lincoln: Nebraska, State Historical Society, 1945), p. 26.

pp. 22–23   "settlers have been most unfortunate . . ." James Mooney. *The Ghost Dance Religion and the Sioux Outbreak of 1890* (Lincoln: University of Nebraska Press, 1991), p. 834.

p. 23   "The teachers had prepared . . ." *Report and Historical Collections Compiled by the South Dakota State Historical Society, XXIX 1958*, pp. 26–28.

p. 24   "There will be a mass meeting . . ." *Black Hills Daily Times,* March 11, 1882.

p. 26   "Last year when . . ." U.S. Senate. *Report of the Sioux Commission of 1889*, 51st Cong., 1st sess., no. 51.

p. 29   "The Sioux reservation contains . . ." Sioux City *Journal*, January 3, 1890.

VISIONS OF PARADISE

3

On New Year's Day 1889, a sudden, terrifying darkness fell across western North America. As the moon moved in front of the sun, the day was slowly blotted out, and the stars and constellations of night began to appear. The Paiute living below in the dry mountain valleys and desert plains of Nevada saw the sky slowly grow dark. While they watched, a member of their tribe, who was suffering from a fever, fell into a trance. He saw a vision of himself being taken up into paradise, where he could see and talk to his long-dead relatives. The land there was watered and green; there were herds of buffalo and antelope grazing on the grassy plains and hills. The Indians were all happy, and none of them were sick or old. War and fighting did not exist, and in this paradise white people were nowhere to be seen.

In his vision, the young Paiute Wovoka saw and spoke to God, who gave him the commandments of a new faith that would replace the traditional beliefs of his people. The Indians must make peace among themselves and stop fighting. They must be honest in all their dealings. They must also practice a new dance. During the dance, they would see the ghosts of their dead relatives and would also experience the vision of paradise. "When the sun died, I went up to heaven," explained Wovoka, "and saw God and all the people who had died a long time ago. God told me to come back and tell my people they must be good and love one another,

31

and not fight, or steal, or lie." Inspired by what he had seen, Wovoka began preaching his new doctrine to the Paiute. The visionary Ghost Dance that Wovoka described was first practiced near his home on the Walker Lake Reservation in Nevada.

Wovoka was already known to the Paiute as a healer and prophet whose father, Tavibo (Numo-tibo'o), had also practiced the shamanistic arts. When Tavibo died, Wovoka joined the family of a white rancher, David Wilson. From the Wilsons, who were devout Christians, Wovoka (sometimes known as Jack Wilson) learned about the Christian heaven, about the life and the prophecies of Jesus Christ, and about the Ten Commandments. Later, while living along Puget Sound, Wovoka also learned the Shaker religion, which was founded by a Squaxin Indian named Squsachtun, or John Slocum. Squsachtun had also gone into a trance while sick, and had also spoken to God. "Before I came alive I saw I was a sinner," he explained to a congregation of his followers.

> [An] angel in heaven said to me, "You must go back and turn alive again on earth." I learned that I must be [a] good Christian man on earth, or will be punished. My soul was told that I must come back and live four days on earth. When I came back, I told my friends, "There is a God. My good friends be Christians. If you all try hard and help me, we shall be better men on earth."

The Shaker religion had spread rapidly among the Puget Sound tribes in the early 1880s. The Squaxin and other tribes who adopted it denied the traditional religious practices of their people. Instead, they believed in Jesus Christ and adopted the heaven and hell learned from the Christian faith. During their long ceremonies, their hands, arms, and heads would shake furiously while a vision of paradise came to them. During their services, the Shakers used crucifixes, candles, and other Christian artifacts. Nevertheless, the government agents banned the new faith and imprisoned its leaders, forcing them to hold their services off the reservation. Wrote James Wickersham, a historian and attorney for the Shaker believers, "The spectacle of an Indian church with Indian officers, preachers, and members, and of houses built by the Indians for church purposes, was too much for the average citizen of Puget Sound, and the Shakers were continually disturbed . . ."

In the spring of 1889, news of Wovoka's prophecies and of his doctrine spread to other tribes living in the West. The Shoshone, who lived near the Paiute, adopted the Ghost Dance soon after Wovoka began describing his vision to his followers. An Arapaho named Nakash visited the prophet, then returned to his band and began teaching the doctrine and the songs he had learned. The Arapaho spread the Ghost Dance to the Gros Ventre and Assiniboine Indians of western Dakota Territory. By letter and by word of mouth, the Ghost Dance then arrived among the Cheyenne and the Lakota of the northern Great Plains.

That summer, a young reservation teacher named Elaine Goodale (later Eastman) was camping out with a group of Lakota Indians. On July 23, she wrote in her diary:

> Later in the night a cry is raised: "A traveler comes!"
> Chasing Crane, on his way home from Rosebud, is
> welcomed with supper and a smoke. He tells a strange
> story of the second appearing of Christ! God, he says,
> has appeared to the Crows! . . . He had been grieved by
> the crying of parents for their dead children, and would
> let the sky down upon the earth and destroy the disobe-
> dient. He was beautiful to look upon, and bore paint as a
> sign of power. Men and women listen to this curious
> tale with apparent credence. A vapor bath is arranged,
> and I fall asleep again to the monotonous rise and fall of
> the accompanying songs.

In the fall of 1889, the Indians at Pine Ridge, Rosebud, and Cheyenne River Reservations held councils to discuss the rumors of the Paiute Messiah. The Lakota chiefs decided to send 11 of their own people to Walker Lake Reservation to meet the prophet and learn for themselves about the Ghost Dance. The travelers were Good Thunder, Yellow Breast, Flat Iron, Broken Arm, Cloud Horse, Yellow Knife, Elk Horn, and Kicks Back from Pine Ridge;

Lakota Indians perform a Ghost Dance in the fall of 1890.   *(Photo by George Trager. From the Minnesota Historical Society)*

Short Bull and Mash-the-Kettle from Rosebud; and Kicking Bear from Cheyenne River.

The group traveled along the spreading network of stagecoach runs and railroad lines that were overrunning their old hunting grounds. After reaching the Fort Hall reservation in Idaho, they were joined by several Shoshone and Bannock Indians, as well as a Cheyenne named Porcupine. They left by train for Salt Lake City and then Nevada, where wagons brought them the rest of the way to Mason Valley. The home of Wovoka lay a few miles northwest of the Walker Lake Agency.

Good Thunder later told Elaine Goodale Eastman:

> I saw him at last, a man of surpassing beauty, with long yellow hair, clad in a blue robe. He did not look at us nor speak, but read our thoughts and answered them without words. I saw the prints of the nails in his hands and feet. He said that the crying of the Indians had sounded loud in his ear. He would come to them tomorrow— [meaning next summer]. Then they would be with him in Elysium, living in skin tents and hunting the buffalo.

Wovoka gave a sermon to the pilgrims, then went into a trance. He awoke and began speaking to the Lakota visitors. He had again journeyed to the spirit world, to receive instruction from God. Soon—in the spring of 1891—the Messiah would return, and the earth would undergo a tremendous upheaval. The paradise Wovoka had seen and visited would finally appear on earth. The whites would disappear, and the dead relatives of the Indians would return to life. The Indians would live forever in peace and plenty. But now, the Indians must stop making war and live with the whites. And they must perform the dance that would bring them the visions of paradise.

When he returned to his home near the Tongue River Agency, the Cheyenne apostle Porcupine was called into the office of the agent, Major Carroll, to describe what he had seen. Porcupine explained that Wovoka

> told us all our dead were to be resurrected; that they were all to come back to earth, and that as the earth was too small for them and us, he would do away with heaven, and make the earth itself large enough to contain us all . . . He spoke to us about fighting, and said that was bad, and we must keep from it; that the earth was to be all good hereafter, and we must all be friends with one another . . . He told us not to quarrel, or fight, nor strike each other, nor shoot one another; that the whites and Indians were to be all one people.

That summer, Porcupine introduced the Ghost Dance to the Cheyenne of the Tongue River Agency. The dance and the Indians were peaceful, but the new ceremony worried settlers and ranchers living near the reservation. "The order went forth that in order to please the Great Spirit a six days and nights' dance must be held every new moon," according to a report written by the commissioner of Indian Affairs.

> With the understanding that at the expiration of a certain period the Great Spirit would restore the buffalo, elk, and other game, resurrect all dead Indians, endow his believers with perpetual youth, and perform many

WHITE RESPONSE TO THE GHOST DANCE

The Ghost Dance was an entirely new faith, one created by Wovoka in response to the destruction of a traditional way of life. Yet for the whites who first confronted the Ghost Dance, it seemed to be a manifestation of defiance and rebellion. The best way to end the Ghost Dance, many agency officials believed, was to simply ignore it. C. C. Warner, the agent at the Walker Lake Reservation, explained his course of action toward the Ghost Dance prophet in a letter to James Mooney, a member of the U.S. Bureau of Ethnology who investigated the Ghost Dance just after the massacre at Wounded Knee.

My Dear Sir: Your letter of September 24 in regard to Jack Wilson [Wovoka], the "Messiah," is at hand and duly noted . . . I do not know as it will be possible to get a photo of him. I never saw him or a photo of him. He works among the whites about 40 miles from my Walker Lake reserve, and never comes near the agency when I visit it . . . I am pursuing the course with him of nonattention or a silent ignoring. He seems to think, so I hear, that I will arrest him should he come within my reach. I would give him no such notoriety. He, like all other prophets, has but little honor in his own country . . . He got his doctrine in part from contact, living in and with a religious family. There are neither ghost songs, dances, nor ceremonials among them about my agencies. Would not be allowed. I think they died out with "Sitting Bull." This is the extent of the information I can give you.

Very respectfully yours,
C. C. Warner, United States Indian Agent.

other wonders . . . Dances . . . were enthusiastically attended, and the accompanying feasts were so associated by stockmen with the disappearance of their cattle that very strained relations resulted between the rancher and Indian, which at one time threatened serious trouble.

Short Bull, Kicking Bear, and the other Lakota visitors had returned to their own homes in March 1890. By this time, the Ghost

Dance was already spreading throughout the mountain region of the West. The Cheyenne, Assiniboine, Mandan, Arikara, Gros Ventre, and Arapaho people all believed in Wovoka's coming Messiah. Ghost Dance camps were built throughout the Great

A leading apostle of the Ghost Dance, Short Bull introduced the ceremony to the Lakota after visiting the Ghost Dance prophet Wovoka. *(Photo by George E. Spencer, Fort Sheridan. From the Minnesota Historical Society)*

Plains and in the northern Rocky Mountains, with each tribe adding songs, incantations, and sermons in its own language and altering the doctrine to fit its own religious traditions.

Other tribes were also hearing of the new faith but ignoring it. The Navajo, who lived in the desert Southwest, learned of the doctrine from a Paiute messenger but paid it little attention. In 1891, several Hopi Indians witnessed a Ghost Dance held by the Havasupai Indians, who lived along Havasupai Creek near the Grand Canyon. The Hopi visitors brought back news of the Ghost Dance to their people, but Wovoka's prophecies did not take hold among them. The Kiowa of the southern Great Plains adopted the Ghost Dance but later abandoned it, as would many other tribes after the troubles that would come to the Lakota reservations.

The Dakota people themselves were divided. The Santee and Yankton who lived in the plains and forests east of the Missouri River did not accept the Ghost Dance, nor did the people of the Crow Creek Reservation, adjacent to Lower Brulé on the river's eastern bank. But after their return from Mason Valley, Short Bull and Kicking Bear found an enthusiastic audience among the Lakota of the Pine Ridge, Rosebud, and Cheyenne River Reservations.

After the false treaties and the loss of their land, the Lakota of these reservations were feeling a growing desperation. General Crook's promises meant nothing to them now—the general had died in March, and the Congress, seeking only to herd the Indians out of the way, had not honored the pledges that he had made. The buffalo were gone, and the crop failures and ration cuts now threatened starvation. A ring of soldiers and army posts surrounded them, making resistance impossible.

The fatal white diseases had struck—at Pine Ridge alone, 45 Oglala were dying every month from influenza, measles, or other sicknesses. When Short Bull and Kicking Bear returned with the news that the whites were to disappear the next spring, and that their green and game-filled hunting grounds were to reappear, many of the Lakota were eager to believe them.

Most of the Rocky Mountain and Plains Indians who adopted the Ghost Dance followed Wovoka's commandments and ceased their raiding and war parties. But by the time the Ghost Dance reached the Lakota, the commandment of Wovoka to keep the peace had been forgotten. Among the followers of Short Bull, Kicking Bear, and other Lakota Ghost Dance leaders, Wovoka's promises of a coming paradise turned into a prophecy of destruction for the whites. And in the coming confrontation, the Ghost Dance believers would have magical protection. In one of his trances, Little Wound met Wovoka's Great Spirit, who told him that

> If the high priests would make for the dancers medicine shirts and pray over them, no harm could come to the wearer; that the bullets of any whites that desired to stop the Messiah Dance would fall to the ground without doing any one harm, and the person firing such shots would drop dead. He said that he had prepared a hole in the ground filled with hot water and fire for the reception of all white men and non-believers . . .

One of the first Lakota bands to take up the Ghost Dance was Chief Big Foot's band of Miniconjou. Big Foot himself, or Sitanka, was a widely respected traditional chief, well-known among the other Lakota leaders for his abilities as a peacemaker. That summer of 1890, Big Foot's diplomacy would be severely tested. While his people began dancing for the destruction of the whites, a group of settlers and ranchers were claiming homesteads on the newly opened land near his camp at the western edge of the Cheyenne River Reservation. The situation soon grew tense; the army had already ordered three troops of cavalry and two companies of infantry to move from Fort Meade in the Black Hills to just off the reservation, near the two main forks of the Cheyenne River.

Suspicious of this new faith and fearing that it would disrupt their agencies, the agents took steps to suppress it. When Short Bull began holding Ghost Dance councils at Rosebud, Agent J. George Wright sent reservation police to attend the councils. After his police made their report, Wright called Short Bull in and ordered him to stop preaching. For the time being, Short Bull complied. At Pine Ridge, Agent Hugh Gallagher had Good Thunder and two other Ghost Dance leaders imprisoned for three days.

Threatening another term in prison, Gallagher ordered the men to stop spreading the Ghost Dance doctrine. He was obeyed.

At Cheyenne River, Kicking Bear wrote to Lakota leaders at the other reservations, inviting them all to a great council to discuss the new religion. But after Wright and Gallagher's intervention, the other chiefs stayed away and the council came to nothing. The Lakota were not yet ready to risk an open confrontation with the agents, who might bring the soldiers out of their forts and onto the reservations. For a time, the Ghost Dance troubles quieted.

But rumors of the Ghost Dance and of trouble among the Lakota were now reaching Washington. The first information had been a letter from Charles L. Hyde, a citizen of Pierre, South Dakota, who had received news of the Ghost Dance from a young Indian friend. Hyde passed on the news to John Noble, secretary of the Department of the Interior, mentioning that "The information has come to me confidentially, through a source I have confidence in, that the Sioux Indians or a portion of them are secretly planning and arranging for an outbreak in the near future . . ."

Noble passed the letter to Robert Belt, the acting commissioner of Indian Affairs, who in turn asked for reports from his agents. McChesney at Cheyenne River, as well as Gallagher, Wright, and McLaughlin, saw no danger that early summer from the Ghost Dance. McLaughlin at Standing Rock did not fear an uprising, but he did associate the new doctrine with those nonprogressive Lakota who opposed him. These "malcontents," as McLaughlin described them, "cling tenaciously to the old Indian ways and are slow to accept the better order of things." To combat the dissension, McLaughlin recommended the arrest of nonprogressive leaders, including Circling Bear, Black Bird, Circling Hawk, and Sitting Bull at his own agency.

In Washington, meanwhile, the House of Representatives had delayed the Indian Appropriation Act for the purchase of annuity goods on the reservations. The appropriation was not officially made until August 19; it also set the budget for rations at $950,000. Food would remain scarce, and the annuity goods, including clothing and tools, would not be distributed until December, when the cold Dakota winter would already be well under way.

NOTES

pp. 31–32   "When the sun died . . ." Mooney, p. 764.

p. 32   "Before I came alive . . ." Mooney, p. 752.

pp. 32–33   "The spectacle of an Indian church . . ." Mooney, p. 758.

p. 33   "Later in the night . . ." Elaine Goodale Eastman, p. 28.

p. 34   "I saw him at last . . ." Elaine Goodale Eastman, p. 31.

p. 35   "told us all our dead were to be resurrected . . ." Mooney, p. 796.

pp. 35–36   "The order went forth . . ." Commissioner of Indian Affairs, *Annual Report 1892*, p. 124.

p. 36   "My Dear Sir . . ." Mooney, p. 767.

p. 39   "If the high priests . . ." James P. Boyd. *Recent Indian Wars, Under the Lead of Sitting Bull, and other Chiefs; With a Full Account of the Messiah Craze, and Ghost Dances* (Philadelphia: Publishers Union, 1892), p. 195.

p. 40   "The information has come to me . . ." Smith, p. 82.

p. 40   "malcontents . . . cling tenaciously . . ." Commissioner of Indian Affairs, *Annual Report 1892*, p. 127.

THE GHOST DANCE TROUBLES

The brief campaign by the agents against the Ghost Dance did not end the faith among the Lakota. On the Pine Ridge Reservation, the Ghost Dance returned and spread quickly in the summer of 1890. Believers fled their homes near the agencies and gathered in dance camps along the narrow tributaries of the White River: Medicine Root Creek, Wounded Knee Creek, White Clay Creek, and Porcupine Creek. Kicking Bear, No Water, and Torn Belly led these camps. Each had a circular dance ring, with a sapling or branch standing in their centers, decorated with cloths or flags. While the Ghost Dance was under way, the leader stood in the center, giving directions, the words of songs and incantations, and encouragement to the dancers.

Years after the Ghost Dance died, an Oglala Lakota woman who lived at one of these camps described what she had seen.

> The ceremony starts toward evening . . . When it is announced, all the people that are going to dance go down to the creek to swim and they take a bark of chokecherry stem and chew it or eat some chokecherry. Some have sweatlodge—they sweat that way. The Ghost Dance was like a Sun Dance, but in the Ghost Dance they form a circle, holding hands, and they sing and dance. They do

this till someone falls or several fall. [They have] some visions of going to heaven and back with a good feeling of having seen their dead relatives, but God does not permit them to look at you because you are not dead.

They wait till they tell what they saw or hear during their trance. The dances usually lasted for four days . . . Children are not allowed to go near the ceremony, so my brothers and I play near the wagons or along the hills or go pick cherries while this is going on. It usually lasts after dark and that is it.

The dance camps became a refuge and a rallying ground for the nonprogressive leaders and their bands. The dance inspired these leaders to stand up to the white agents and to the Indian police. On August 24, Pine Ridge agent Hugh Gallagher rode out to Torn Belly's Ghost Dance camp on White Clay Creek. Gallagher's presence about quickly brought about a tense standoff between hostile warriors and his own Indian police. The intercession of Young Man Afraid of His Horses saved the agent's party from a violent confrontation; Torn Belly then invited Gallagher to stay and witness the ceremony for himself. After observing the Ghost Dance, the agent decided to quit interfering and leave the problem to his successor, who would soon be officially appointed by the new administration in Washington.

Most of the people of the Crow Creek and Lower Brulé Reservations, where farming and white civilization were making more progress, rejected the Ghost Dance. But at Lower Brulé, a small group of Lakota did take up Wovoka's religion. When the agent at the Lower Brulé Agency heard of it, he ordered the arrest of 22 Ghost Dancers, who were shipped off the reservation to Fort Snelling in Minnesota. The Ghost Dance did return to the Brulé of Rosebud under the direction of Short Bull, Crow Dog, and Two Strike, and to Hump's band at Cheyenne River. Meanwhile, to show his defiance of the whites and of the new reservation boundaries they had set for him, Big Foot moved his people west and off the Cheyenne River Reservation entirely.

In October, Kicking Bear brought the Ghost Dance to the Hunkpapa of Standing Rock. At his camp on Grand River, Sitting Bull

Kicking Bear brought the Ghost Dance to Sitting Bull and to Big Foot's Miniconjou band. *(Photo by George E. Spencer, Fort Sheridan. From the Minnesota Historical Society)*

gave his approval to the religion, seeing in it a way to further undermine the authority of the Standing Rock agent. Although McLaughlin ordered his police to escort Kicking Bear off the reservation, the Hunkpapa soon became devoted adherants to the new faith. To resolve the conflict, Sitting Bull asked McLaughlin to accompany him to Nevada, where the two men could talk to the Messiah in person and then decide what to do. McLaughlin refused.

By October 1890 Agent McLaughlin was growing more alarmed over the Ghost Dance. McLaughlin feared that Sitting Bull would make use of the doctrine in his ongoing campaign against the white agents and the progressive camp. In a letter to the commissioner of Indian Affairs, the agent reported that the Indians of his reservation now believed that "the dead are all returning to reinhabit this earth, which belongs to the Indian; that they are driving back with them, as they return, immense herds of buffalo, and elegant wild horses to have for the catching; that the Great Spirit . . . is now with them and against the whites, and will cover the earth over with thirty feet of additional soil, well sodded and timbered, under which the whites will all be smothered, and any whites who escape these great phenomena will become small fishes in the rivers of the country. . . ." McLaughlin went on to say: "Sitting Bull is high priest and leading apostle of this latest Indian absurdity; in a word he is chief mischief-maker at this agency, and if he were not here, this craze, so general among the Sioux, would never have gotten a foothold. . . ." McLaughlin again recommended to the commissioner of Indian Affairs that Sitting Bull be arrested and imprisoned for the winter. Without Sitting Bull present to stir up trouble, McLaughlin believed he could handle the situation without troops, as the hunger and cold of winter would lessen resistance toward his police.

Meanwhile, new agents were arriving on the Lakota reservations. Under the system of political spoils and patronage, agent's jobs were being rewarded to supporters of the newly elected Republican administration and Congress. In 1885, the Democrats had used the patronage system to replace 50 out of the 58 reservation agents. Now, in 1890, it was the turn of the Republican party and of the new South Dakota senators, Richard Pettigrew and Gideon C. Moody.

Pettigrew, who had sought and won a seat on the Senate committee for Indian Affairs, began appointing his South Dakota Republican allies to run the Lakota reservations. The appointees began arriving at the agencies in October 1890. Agent Wright was replaced by E. B. Reynolds, who immediately was confronted with mounting hostility among the Ghost Dancers led by Short Bull. Unsure of how to handle the Ghost Dance, which reminded many whites of an Indian war dance, Reynolds reported an imminent outbreak and began calling for troops to keep the peace at his agency.

At Pine Ridge, Hugh Gallagher was replaced on October 9 by Daniel F. Royer, a pharmacist and leading citizen from the small South Dakota town of Alpena. Royer had no experience whatsoever in the Indian Bureau or in dealing with the Lakota. But he did have the strong support of Senator Pettigrew. While the Senate considered the agency appointment in the spring of 1890, Pettigrew had written to Royer to issue instructions and outline his strategy for managing the reservation: "I have filed a letter endorsing you for Pine Ridge. If you secure the appointment I shall want to clean out the whole force of farmers, teachers, and clerks as far as possible and put in Dakota men. You can not make an appointment until you consult Moody and I about it."

For several years, Hugh Gallagher had been able to handle the agency with the help of the Oglala police force established by Valentine McGillycuddy. Gallagher and McGillycuddy, who now lived in Rapid City, were both proud to have never needed the assistance or advice of the U.S. Army or of the War Department. Royer, however, soon found that he could not manage the Lakota in his charge or his own police force. On October 12, soon after arriving at Pine Ridge, he sent his first telegram to the Indian Bureau asking for the protection and support of the military. Commissioner Robert Belt, seeking to keep the Department of War away from management of the reservations, denied the request.

South Dakota's newspapers soon got wind of the troubles at the agencies and, in the interest of selling an exciting story to their readers, began whipping up fear of an Indian uprising. Joseph Gossage, editor of the Rapid City *Journal*, offered his own interpretation of the Ghost Dance faith on September 25:

> Reliable parties just in from the interior of the reservation state that many bands of Indians are daily looking for the coming of Christ . . . He is to cover the earth with another stratum of soil thirty feet deep, burying everyone but faithful Indians, who will squirm through on top to find grass waist high. Plenty of wild horses will roam around and not a paleface will be seen. . . .

At Pine Ridge, the rising religious fervor among the Oglala led to more confrontations between agency police and the Ghost Dance believers. With Agent Royer's alarming telegrams circulating through the government, the War Department decided to investigate. On October 27, General Miles, now commander of the Department of the Missouri, arrived at Pine Ridge. At a council with the Oglala chiefs, he asked that the Ghost Dance be stopped and that the hostile bands desert their camps away from the agency. The Ghost Dance leaders refused to take the general's advice; later they simply laughed at Royer when the agent made the same suggestion.

After Miles left Pine Ridge, Royer wrote to Commissioner Belt: "I . . . have brought all the persuasion to bear on the leaders that was possible but without effect and the only remedy for this matter is the use of military . . ." The nervous agent, whom the Oglalas dubbed Lakotah Kopegla Koskala, or Young Man Afraid of Lakotas, was now demanding 600 troops to help him keep the peace.

White alarm over the Ghost Dance simply fortified the dance leaders. They had surrendered most of their land and many freedoms, but they believed that the Lakota still had a right to a religion—especially one that adopted the tenets of the white man's own. Shortly after Miles's visit, Short Bull gave an angry sermon to Ghost Dance believers at Red Leaf's camp, declaring

I will soon start this thing in running order. I have told you that this will come to pass in two seasons, but since the whites are interfering so much, I will advance the time from what my father above told me to do, and the time will be shorter . . . You must not be afraid of anything. The guns are the only things we are afraid of, but they belong to our father in heaven. He will see that they do no harm.

Ghost shirts were often worn by dancers during the Ghost Dance ceremony. Among the Lakota, the shirts were said to prevent harm from the bullets of the white soldiers. *(South Dakota State Historical Society, Pierre)*

Oglala and Brulé dancers then gathered at the mouth of Pass Creek, on White River near the border of Pine Ridge and Rosebud Reservations. There Short Bull was joined by Kicking Bear, as the Lakota at the camp began trading their horses for guns and ammunition.

On October 31, President Harrison ordered the War Department to carry out another investigation of the troubled Lakota reservations. Brigadier General Thomas H. Ruger, commander of the Department of Dakota, left for Standing Rock Reservation, where he met with Agent McLaughlin. Ruger and McLaughlin agreed that the arrest of Sitting Bull might help solve the crisis. Instead of calling in troops, however, McLaughlin would employ reservation police to make the arrest, and Ruger would allow McLaughlin to decide on the right moment. Ruger also ordered reinforcements to Fort Bennett, the post lying just south of Cheyenne River Agency along the Missouri River, to prevent any trouble from the villages of Hump or Big Foot.

With winter approaching, and their rations and annuities reduced, the Indians greatly feared the hunger and cold that was soon to come. By promising a paradise in the spring, Short Bull and other Ghost Dance leaders attracted a wide audience, and the stage was set for a violent confrontation on the reservation. On November 10, Oglala and Brulé were still leaving the agencies for Ghost Dance camps. Royer begged to be allowed to come to Washington to explain his difficulties; Belt advised him to stay at his post.

On November 12, the gathering storm nearly broke during a ration issue at the Pine Ridge Agency. While the Ghost Dance camps were coming in for their rations, reservation police attempted to arrest Little, an Oglala accused of killing a steer without permission. Quickly surrounded by hostile Oglala, the police were forced to retreat without their prisoner. A fight was narrowly avoided through the intervention of Chief American Horse. "Stop! Think! What are you going to do?" American Horse cried out during the confrontation. "Kill these men of our own race? Then what? Kill all these helpless white men, women, and children.

And what then? What will these brave words, brave deeds lead to in the end? How long can you hold out? Your country is surrounded . . ."

"It seems to me as I recall the incident that this man's voice had almost magic power," wrote Charles Eastman, who was present in his agency physician's office. "It is likely that he saved us all from a massacre, for the murder of the police, who represented the authority of the Government, would surely have been followed by a general massacre."

Also witnessing the attempted arrest of Little was Agent Royer, who cowered in his office while American Horse calmed the situation in the street. Royer immediately sent another wire: "I deem the situation at this agency very critical, and believe that an outbreak may occur at any time, and it does not seem to me to be safe to any longer withhold troops." Royer then fled to Rushville, Nebraska, just south of the reservation boundary.

Royer's telegrams, and a warning of impending trouble on the reservations by Secretary of the Interior Noble, prompted President Harrison to take action on November 14. Harrison ordered the secretary of war to take steps to prevent the widely feared Indian outbreak. On November 15, Royer returned to Pine Ridge and cabled Belt: "Indians are dancing in the snow and are wild and crazy . . . We need protection and we need it now. I have submitted to you the result of six weeks calm conservative investigation and nothing short of 1000 soldiers will settle this dancing."

On November 17, the army swung into action. General Miles ordered Brigadier General John Brooke, commander of the Department of the Platte, to send troops to Pine Ridge and Rosebud Agencies and to deploy cavalry units along railroad and telegraph lines in the vicinity of the southern reservations. Miles was eager to prove his point that the War Department could better handle the reservations than could the Interior and the Indian Bureau. The army would move swiftly and decisively; an overwhelming show of force would soon calm the situation. Miles reminded Brooke that he must not allow his officers or enlisted men to mix

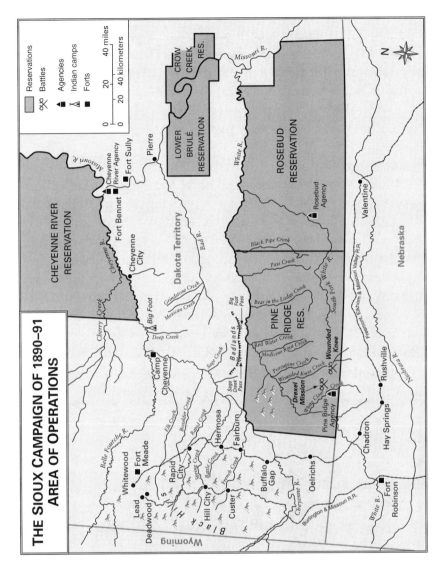

A major cause of the Ghost Dance fighting was the perceived threat of hostile reservation Lakota to white settlers living along the tributaries of the Cheyenne River (left of map).

with the Indians. To avoid confrontation as much as possible, or heavy losses in any fight that might break out, Miles wanted the soldiers kept at a distance. The general repeated the order several times during the next few weeks.

Miles's strategy was to isolate the hostile Ghost Dance camps and persuade their leaders to come into the agencies peacefully. He would have the most prominent Ghost Dance leaders arrested, but he would also try to avoid any fighting with the Lakota. The warriors numbered around 5,000 and were still well armed; Miles also knew that the war parties could seize plenty of horses and cattle from the farms and ranches surrounding the reservation in case of an outbreak.

From Fort Robinson, the soldiers marched to Valentine and Rushville, along the Fremont, Elkhorn, and Missouri Valley Railroad. Brooke ordered a night march from the two rail stops to take the Lakota by surprise and to avoid any confrontations. The troops set out on the night of November 19 to the agencies, with Brooke himself leading three troops of the Ninth Cavalry, four companies of the Second Infantry, one company of the Eighth Infantry, as well as a Hotchkiss cannon and a Gatling gun, from Rushville to Pine Ridge Agency. After arriving in the early morning of November 20, Brooke also recruited two troops of Oglala scouts. From Valentine, Lieutenant Colonel A. T. Smith marched at the head of two troops of the Ninth Cavalry, three companies

After a night march to Pine Ridge, U.S. troops made their camp along the streets of the Pine Ridge Agency. The agency was also the site of General Brooke's command post. *(South Dakota State Historical Society, Pierre)*

of the Eighth Infantry, and a Hotchkiss battery to Rosebud. More troops would arrive from Kansas, Wyoming, Montana, and New Mexico; units were also held in reserve at Fort Leavenworth, Kansas. It was the largest muster of the U.S. Army since the Civil War.

"I remember seeing the soldiers from the East coming in by train, to the small siding about a quarter of a mile from our house," wrote a young white settler named Sarah Jane Osborne.

> They brought their horses with them and next day began their march into the Indian country. My husband took a wagon load of supplies to the soldiers' camp, which was about thirty miles away and out little son aged ten years went with him. They saw by the side of the trail many dead cattle. The Indians had killed them and carried a portion of the meat away with them for food, in their hurry to get to their retreat in the "Bad Lands."

Brooke immediately sent out agency police to ask the Oglala at the Ghost Dance camps to come in to the agency, where he promised they would be fed and held safe from any harm. Miles and Brooke believed that the show of military strength would convince the Indians to obey their orders. But the army tents, artillery pieces, and blue uniforms had exactly the opposite effect on many of the Oglala. "Ponies were hurriedly caught and watered, tents razed, goods packed, and soon two long files of wagons moved in opposite directions," recalled Elaine Goodale Eastman. "While the 'church party' and most non-dancers sadly obeyed orders, the dancers, fearing summary punishment, fled in panic to the natural fortress of the Bad Lands."

Ghost Dance leaders brought their followers as far as possible away from the soldiers and the agencies. Big Road, No Water, and Little Wound moved to the mouth of White Clay Creek. Short Bull camped along Pass Creek. Two Strike and several other Brulé leaders and their followers fled the Rosebud Reservation and moved west to Pine Ridge, with Two Strike's group stopping along Wounded Knee Creek. Meanwhile, General Brooke was reinforced at Pine Ridge Agency by four companies of the Second Infantry, a troop of the Ninth Cavalry, and the Seventh Cavalry

Regiment, which had suffered the defeat at the Little Bighorn River. Now under the command of Colonel James Forsyth, a man with no experience in conflict with the Lakota, the Seventh set up camp to watch and guard the Oglala and Brulé warriors some of whom had helped to defeat George Armstrong Custer 14 years before. The infantry built trenches and defense works along the agency streets; soldiers patrolled the area day and night. A curfew was enforced, while Lakota children were locked into their boarding school to ensure the obedience of their parents.

Within the next few days, the promises of General Brooke, and the persuasion of agency scouts, had convinced several of the Oglala chiefs at White Clay Creek, including Big Road and Little Wound, to surrender and come in to Pine Ridge Agency. On Thanksgiving Day, November 27, Brooke ordered a full ration issue for the Lakota at the agency. Meanwhile, General Miles had convinced the Harrison administration that martial law on the Lakota reservations was necessary. On December 1, the secretary of the interior ordered the agents to follow instructions of the military commanders. The army now had full responsibility for managing the Ghost Dance troubles.

At the mouth of Pass Creek, Short Bull sent messengers to Two Strike, to Kicking Bear, and to Sitting Bull, inviting all the Ghost Dance leaders to gather in the Badlands and begin preparing for the coming of the Messiah. On November 30, Two Strike's Brulé rampaged through homes and ranches along Wounded Knee Creek, setting fire to cabins and making off with the Pine Ridge Agency cattle herd. The band joined Short Bull and Kicking Bear on December 1. Now including about 3,000 Oglala and Brulé, the group made its way northwest to the Badlands, where it occupied a high, steep, and easily defended neck of land known as the Stronghold.

The presence of a large body of armed Lakota in the Stronghold greatly worried white settlers in the area as well as Brooke and Miles, who knew that their outnumbered soldiers would not be able to capture the site. Miles ordered the Stronghold surrounded. Colonel Eugene Carr and eight troops of the Sixth Cavalry took

COWBOY BERRY'S TALL TALE

The Ghost Dance was spreading, leading perhaps to another Indian campaign on the frontier. Settlers in western Dakota heard frightening rumors and told bloodcurdling war stories. The following passage takes place in "An 1890 War Time Story," written by a South Dakota pioneer named Rena Murphy, and is part of an unpublished manuscript titled *Indian and Pioneer Stories* in the South Dakota State Archives:

Indians, white men and women, and even we younger folk took a thrilling part in the happenings of these war-scare days. Indians had been scouting out of their Reservation at night and stealing horses and cattle. The beef was jerked (cut in long strips and dried in the sun) for winter use, and the horses were trained for war service.

The Indians expected to repeat the Little Big Horn battle, that battle which took the lives of General Custer and all of his dashing cavalry. All of this is American history and my story is of facts and things that happened around that time.

In the fall of 1890 our neighborhood had a school house gathering, our literary society. During the meeting a cowboy known as Cowboy Berry (all cowboys of early days had a special name or nickname) had just come from near the Indian camp so had news from the front.

In order to add romance to his story he related that the Indians were in full war paint and had their guns stacked like corn fodder shocks, and with glaring campfires were dancing and singing war cries. It put a scare into our little assembly as the Indians were less than forty miles away.

. . . For days settlers rushed away from their homes. Some hardly waited to gather up their children so frightened were they. It was reported that some children were actually left behind, but that they were rescued by other fleeing ranchers.

Actually the Indians were not as near as reported and brave western men were on the alert day and night. Now you see how the story of this young cowboy meant only for a joke was the start of a general stampede. Most important all escaped the savages and their scalping knives.

Later, when the scare was over and the truth had become known, Cowboy Berry was with me at the roadside when Joe Foreman, who had made the dash for his niece on the frontier, and who had spread the alarm about the Indians on the warpath, drove along the road. Cowboy Berry had to make a quick getaway to avoid a thrashing . . .

up a position at the mouth of Rapid Creek, to the west. Lieutenant Colonel George Sanford marched four cavalry troops from Fort Leavenworth to a camp along the Cheyenne River. Seven companies of the 17th Infantry, under Lieutenant Colonel R. H. Offley, patrolled farther downriver to prevent the Lakota of the northern reservations from joining the hostiles in the Stronghold. Army scouts probed into the Badlands, searching for Lakota who might be roaming toward the Cheyenne River settlements.

Nevertheless, the Lakota in the Badlands remained peaceful. According to Commissioner Morgan's report, "Groups of Indians from the different reservations had commenced concentrating in the Badlands, upon or in the vicinity of the Pine Ridge reservation. Killing of cattle and destruction of other property by these Indians . . . occurred . . . but no signal fires were built, no warlike demonstrations were made, no violence was done to any white settlers, nor was there any cohesion or organization among the Indians themselves. Many of them were friendly Indians who had never participated in the Ghost Dance, but had fled thither from fear of soldiers . . ."

Meanwhile, newspaper reporters from around the country were assembled at Pine Ridge Agency, prepared for the worst. The Rapid City *Journal* warned: "Dispatches from the Cheyenne Agency say the Messiah dances are still the order of the day . . . Major McLaughlin, Agent at Standing Rock, admits that the Indians are now beyond his control. Sitting Bull told him a day or two ago that the braves had no use for him and would shortly wipe the whites out entirely." Anxious for a good story to report, many of them grew critical of the patient strategy of Miles and Brooke. The *Black Hills Daily Times* asked,

> What are they [the Army] doing? So far as the dis-
> patches show, nothing. The Indians continue to dance
> and defy the soldiers, and even to defy them to fight,
> and declare that they will dance to their heart's con-
> tent . . . In the name of all that is sensible, why were
> these soldiers moved from all quarters of this continent
> if not to subdue this insolence of a savage race, to take

their arms from them, to stop their infernal ghost dancing, and allay the fears of the timid frontiersman?

The *Pierre Free Press*, however, offered a different angle on
the story:

> If ever a stupendous fake was better faked . . . please tell
> us about it! It is when one approaches the alleged scenes
> of hostility that he begins to comprehend the dimen-
> sions of the grand farce. After getting into hostile coun-
> try the visitor becomes so disgusted with the utter lack
> of signs of hostility that he becomes ugly himself, and a
> disposition to shoot something is almost irresistable.

Frightened by the rumors and the false reports, the citizens of
small towns near the reservations began organizing home militias
to deal with the promised outbreak. The town of Buffalo Gap, west
of the Badlands, raised a force of 40 men and sent pickets out east
of town. Oelrichs, Hot Springs, and Rapid City also organized
volunteer companies and wired Governor Mellette for arms. The
panic spread throughout the state and to towns several hundred
miles distant from the Lakota. The commissioner of Indian Affairs reported:

> In another city, a place of 3,000 inhabitants, 75 miles
> from any Indians and 150 miles from any hostiles, word
> came about 2 o'clock Sunday morning for the militia to
> be in readiness. The company promptly assembled,
> were instructed and drilled. In an evening church serv-
> ice one of the pastors broke out in prayer: "O Lord, pre-
> pare us for what awaits us. We have just been listening
> to the sweet sounds of praise, but ere the morning sun
> we may hear the war whoop of the red man." The effect
> on children and nervous persons may be imagined . . .

Trying to calm the citizens, Mellette wrote a "Proclamation" on
November 28 that stated:

> In view of the widespread alarm for fear of an Indian
> outbreak, I can assure all settlers east of the Missouri

A NEWSPAPERMAN'S ACCOUNT

Frederic Remington was a well-known artist who also worked as a journalist during the Ghost Dance troubles. Sent west by Harper's Weekly magazine to cover the story, Remington witnessed many important events during the army's mobilization to the Lakota reservations. Although the military distrusted journalists, the two leaders of the campaign, Miles and Brooke, saw in Remington a source of valuable publicity, as Remington was decidedly proarmy when it came to Indian conflicts. The dramatic language of his dispatches was also intended to fascinate and thrill *Harper's* readers with tales of adventure on the dangerous, and thankfully distant, western frontier.

The following excerpt is from a short Remington article entitled "The Art of War and Newspaper Men," printed in the December 6, 1890 edition of *Harper's Weekly*.

> Less than two weeks ago I passed over the trail from Rushville, Nebraska, to the Pine Ridge Agency behind Major-General Nelson Miles. Tonight the moon is shining as it did then, but it will go down in the middle of the night, and I can see in my mind's eye the Second Infantry and the Ninth Troopers, with their trains of wagons, plodding along in the dark. The distance

River that they are in no possible danger, and I urge them to remain quietly on their farms attending to their ordinary labors. . . . Every alarming rumor with any foundation has been traced to its source and was found to be absolutely groundless. No act, or even word of hostility, has been spoken or committed by any Indian, anywhere.

But on December 4, after the Ghost Dancers had rampaged through the Pine Ridge ranches and occupied the Stronghold, Mellette began issuing rifles and ammunition to the volunteer militias.

Satisfied that the Lakota in the Stronghold were now the only remaining hostiles he had to deal with, Brooke prepared to negotiate indirectly with them. He gave permission for Father John Jutz, priest of the Holy Rosary Mission on Pine Ridge, to ride out is twenty-eight miles, and at four o'clock in the morning they will arrive. When the Ogallalas view the pine-clad bluffs they will see in the immediate foreground a large number of Sibley tents, and, being warriors, they will know that each Sibley has eighteen men in it. They will be much surprised. They will hold little impromptu councils, and will probably seek for the motive of this concentration of troops. And some man will say: "Well, the soldiers are here, and if your people don't keep quiet—Well, you know what soldiers are for." The Ogallalas will understand why the soldiers are there without any further explanation. There may be and probably will be some white friend of the Indians who can tell them something they do not know. A little thing has happened since the Ogallalas laid their arms down, and that is that the bluecoats in the Second Infantry can put a bullet into the anatomy of an Ogallala at one thousand yards' range with almost absolute certainty if the light is fair and the wind not too strong.

I must not try to prophesy what the Ogallalas will do when they see the Sibleys, but I hope the friend will be there to tell them what a regular soldier and a Long Tom can do. The days when they could circle like hawks about a rabbit are gone. The modern United States soldier can pile a pony up in a heap before its rider can go one hundred yards. I realize that before this matter is printed the biggest Indian war since 1758 will be in progress, or that the display of military force will have accomplished its object, and the trouble gone . . .

to the Stronghold and try to persuade the Lakota to come in to the agency. Accompanied by Jack Red Cloud, the Oglala chief's son, Jutz set out for the Stronghold on December 3. On the next day, he reached the camp and began talking with Two Strike and the other leaders. By dawn on December 5, Jutz had convinced Two Strike and several other chiefs to accompany him to Pine Ridge Agency to meet with Brooke. The priest had succeeded only after promising that the Ghost Dance leaders could kill him if the whites attacked.

The group filed into the agency the next day. Brooke, who had just convinced the War Department to make up the ration shortage, made a strong case for surrender, promising that the Ghost Dancers and their leaders would not be arrested or harmed. "The agent will forgive you if you come in now," Brooke told them, "and he will also increase your rations. The only restriction is that you may not do the ghost dance." Still defiant and distrustful, the chiefs would only agree to return to the Stronghold to consider their next action.

Brooke then sent a scout named Louis Shangreau to the Stronghold with a message urging the Lakota to come in peacefully. This time, Short Bull flatly refused, saying

> If the Great Father would permit us to continue the dance, would give more rations, and quit taking away portions of the reservation, I would be in favor of returning. But even if you say that he will, how can we discern whether you are telling the truth? We have been lied to so many times that we will not believe any words that your agent sends us . . . We prefer to stay here and die, if necessary, to loss of liberty . . . We tell you to return to your agent and say to him that the Dakotas in the Bad Lands are not going to come in.

The Ghost Dance continued in the Stronghold for two more days. On December 10, however, Two Strike and Crow Dog changed their minds. They would accept Brooke's promises and would go to the agency. When Short Bull spoke against this surrender, a violent melee began, in which Shangreau and the small group of Oglala scouts and agency police who had accompanied him grappled with several hundred angry warriors. Ashamed of this fighting among his own people, Crow Dog sat on the ground and pulled a blanket over his head, a gesture of despair that immediately calmed the situation. Two Strike and Crow Dog left the Stronghold with most of the Lakota. Kicking Bear and Short Bull started out with them but soon returned to the Stronghold with a few hundred Ghost Dancers who were not yet ready to give up.

The situation at Pine Ridge Reservation appeared to be coming to a standoff, with the hostile group now just a small gathering in a distant, surrounded spot. Believing that diplomacy would not convince the remaining dancers to come in, Brooke proposed an all-out attack on the Stronghold. Carr and the Sixth Cavalry would take up positions north of the Stronghold, while Brooke would lead the assault from the south with troops from the Pine Ridge Agency. General Miles denied Brooke's plans and ordered instead a blockade of the Stronghold with three cavalry columns. Miles would use the cold weather and hunger to bring Kicking Bear and Short Bull and their followers to surrender.

On December 15, as Two Strike, Crow Dog, and their followers began arriving at Pine Ridge Agency, the situation appeared to be calming down. But as the next day dawned, the Lakota heard bad news from the Standing Rock Reservation. At the Grand River settlement, Agent McLaughlin's Indian police had arrived at Sitting Bull's cabin to place the Hunkpapa leader under arrest. The result had been a violent struggle in which many Indians, including Ghost Dancers, policemen, and Sitting Bull himself, had been killed.

NOTES

pp. 42–43 "The ceremony starts toward evening . . ." Renee S. Flood. *Lost Bird of Wounded Knee: Spirit of the Lakota* (New York: Scribner, 1995), p. 10.

p. 45 "the dead are all returning . . ." Commissioner of Indian Affairs, *Annual Report 1892*, p. 125.

p. 46 "I have filed a letter . . ." Pettigrew letter to Royer, quoted in Philip S. Hall. *To Have This Land: The Nature of Indian/White Relations, South Dakota, 1888–1891* (Vermilion: University of South Dakota Press, 1991), p. 16.

p. 47 "Reliable parties just in . . ." Rapid City *Journal*, September 25, 1890.

p. 47 "I . . . have brought . . ." Robert M. Utley. *The Last Days of the Sioux Nation* (New Haven: Yale University Press, 1963), p. 109.

p. 48 "I will soon start this thing . . ." Mooney, pp. 788–789.

pp. 49–50 "Stop! Think! . . ." Utley, p. 108.

p. 50 "It seems to me . . ." Dr. Charles A. Eastman, p. 95.

p. 50   "Indians are dancing in the snow . . ." Commissioner of Indian Affairs, *Annual Report 1892*, p. 128.

p. 53   "I remember seeing . . ." Sarah Jane Osborne manuscript, South Dakota State Archives.

p. 53   "Ponies were hurriedly caught . . ." Elaine Goodale Eastman, p. 33.

p. 55   "Indians, white men . . ." Rena Murphy manuscript, South Dakota State Archives.

p. 56   "Groups of Indians . . ." Mooney, p. 852.

p. 56   "Dispatches from the Cheyenne Agency . . ." Rapid City *Journal*, November 20, 1890.

pp. 56–57 "What are they . . ." *Black Hills Daily Times*, November 26, 1890.

p. 57   "If ever a stupendous fake . . ." *Pierre Free Press*, November 28, 1890.

p. 57   "In another city . . ." Mooney, p. 892.

pp. 57–58 "In view of the widespread alarm . . ." Hall, p. 69.

pp. 58–59 "Less than two weeks ago . . ." Frederic Remington "The Art of War and Newspaper Men," *Harper's Weekly*, December 6, 1890.

pp. 59–60 "The agent will forgive you . . ." Smith, p. 143.

p. 60   "If the Great Father would . . ." Boyd, p. 208.

THE FIGHT
AT GRAND
RIVER

To the white agents and generals, Sitting Bull represented the greatest threat to peace and progress on the Lakota reservations. The Hunkpapa leader would not sign treaties or surrender the traditions of the Lakota, and he would not accept the settled, agricultural life that whites and progressive Lakota held out as the only chance for the Indians to survive. Sitting Bull still had a large following of supporters at his camp along the Grand River, and he still commanded respect and loyalty on the other Lakota reservations. But he also had made many enemies among the progressives and among the members of the Standing Rock police force.

By the fall of 1890, Agent McLaughlin and General Miles had agreed that Sitting Bull must be arrested and removed from Standing Rock. A large group of armed men would probably be necessary, but using the military stationed at nearby Fort Yates to make the arrest would be dangerous. If the leader of the Hunkpapa decided to resist, his people would fight to protect him. The result would be a bloody shootout that could grow into a general outbreak—precisely what Miles wanted to avoid.

Miles decided on a different plan of action. In late November, without consulting McLaughlin, he decided to engage William D.

Sitting Bull would not accept treaties or assimilation with the whites. He represented the most serious threat to the white agents in their drive to "civilize" the
Lakota. *(Photo from Archive Photos)*

"Buffalo Bill" Cody, a civilian and an old acquaintance, to do the job quietly. Cody knew Sitting Bull personally and had once hired the chief to appear in his Wild West shows. A small group of friendly civilians would have a better chance of success than a larger group of hostile police or white troops, and Miles believed Cody was one white man who could persuade Sitting Bull to come along peacefully. Accordingly, he wrote out an order to Cody to "secure the person of Sitting Bull and deliver him to the nearest com'g officer of U.S. Troops, taking a receipt and reporting your action." Eager for the adventure and for the publicity that would come with it, Cody immediately accepted Miles's commission. Setting out from Chicago on November 24, he reached Bismarck, North Dakota, and then Fort Yates on the 27th. Traveling with him was a small entourage of several friends and newspaper reporters.

At Standing Rock, however, neither Lieutenant Colonel William Drum, commander of Fort Yates, nor Agent McLaughlin were feeling cooperative or hospitable toward Buffalo Bill. McLaughlin did not appreciate his authority being usurped by these peremptory orders; to both men, Cody's commission was nothing more than a dangerous publicity stunt that could get people on both sides hurt or killed. The two men quickly worked out a plan to thwart Cody's mission. While Cody settled and made the acquaintance of Drum and his officers at Fort Yates, McLaughlin sent an urgent wire to the commissioner of Indian Affairs: "Buffalo Bill has arrived here with a commission from General Miles to arrest Sitting Bull. Such a step at present would be unnecessary and unwise, as it will precipitate a fight which can be averted . . . Request Gen. Miles's order to Cody be rescinded and request immediate answer."

In the meantime, the men of Fort Yates carried out their instructions from Drum: ply the old showman with whiskey and cause him a hangover that would prevent any expedition to Sitting Bull's camp. But through the evening and into the night, Cody stood up well enough. "Colonel Cody's capacity," wrote Captain A. R. Chapman, "was such that it took practically all the officers, in details of two or three, to keep him interested and busy."

On the morning of the 28th, Buffalo Bill set out with his party along one of the two trails that led southward to the Grand River camp. That night, while Cody and his party camped, McLaughlin sent scouts along each of the trails with instructions to intercept the party. The next morning, Cody met scout Louis Primeau and stopped to explain his mission. "Well, you're too late," Primeau told Buffalo Bill. "Sitting Bull has gone into the agency with [Standing Rock schoolteacher] Jack Carignan. They went over the other trail." A skeptical Cody then rode over to the other trail, where he found the fresh tracks of two horses and a buggy, heading north, that McLaughlin's scouts had planted the day before. Cody then turned back to Fort Yates, where Drum showed him a new set of instructions from Washington: "The order for the detention of Sitting Bull has been rescinded. You are hereby ordered to return to Chicago and report to General Miles. Benjamin Harrison, President." Disappointed but outmaneuvered, Cody returned east.

McLaughlin and Drum had succeeded in turning away Buffalo Bill, but they still had to make the arrest of Sitting Bull. Now, as General Brooke was negotiating with Short Bull and other Ghost Dance leaders in the Badlands, Sitting Bull was preparing to answer an invitation from the dancers to join them. McLaughlin, who had heard of Sitting Bull's preparation for the journey to Pine Ridge, decided to move ahead with the arrest. On December 5, he wired the Indian Bureau, requesting permission to proceed.

The bureau was still feuding with the War Department over the management of the reservations but had acknowledged military control during the Ghost Dance crisis. The commissioner advised McLaughlin to wait. Army officials then took the time to proceed through proper channels. On December 10, General Miles asked General Ruger to order Drum to make the arrest. M. Barber, Ruger's assistant adjutant general, wired these instructions to Drum on December 12: "The division commander has directed that you make it your especial duty to secure the person of Sitting Bull. Call on Indian agent to cooperate and render such assistance as will best promote the purpose in view . . ." Drum and

McLaughlin now planned to arrest Sitting Bull on the 20th—a ration day, when most of the Hunkpapa would be at the agency. While McLaughlin prepared, Sitting Bull considered the best time for his departure for Pine Ridge and the Stronghold.

General Nelson Miles believed the civilian agents incapable of properly handling the reservations or traditional chiefs such as Sitting Bull. *(Photo from Archive Photos)*

On December 14, McLaughlin's plans were upset by a message from Jack Carignan, who lived a few miles from Sitting Bull's camp. According to reports Carignan heard from Bullhead, a member of the Indian police, Sitting Bull had decided to leave for the Badlands on the morning of the next day. At this moment, the chief and his followers were readying their horses and wagons for the 200-mile journey to Short Bull's dance camp in the Stronghold.

After consulting with Drum, McLaughlin arranged to make the arrest immediately. A force of agency police would rendezvous that night near Sitting Bull's camp, while troops from Fort Yates would march to the vicinity to lend support, if needed. Drum assigned troops F and G of the Eighth Cavalry, under the command of Captain E. G. Fechet, to the mission. Fechet also brought a Hotchkiss cannon, a frightening artillery piece that could hurl two-pound shells at a rapid rate. Guided by Louis Primeau, the troops set out around midnight.

Early the next morning, well before dawn, Bullhead gathered 39 police and four volunteers at the house of Grey Eagle, the brother-in-law of Sitting Bull. At about five o'clock, the force set out for Sitting Bull's house. One of the police, John Lone Man, recalled that:

> We rode in a dogtrot gait till we got about a mile from the camp, then we galloped along and when we were about a quarter of a mile, we rode up as if we attacked the camp. Upon our arrival at Sitting Bull's cabin, we quickly dismounted and while the officers went inside we all scattered round the cabin.
> Bullhead, followed by Red Tomahawk and Shavehead, knocked at the door and the Chief answered "How, hiyu wo," "All right, come in." The door was opened and Bullhead said, "I come after you to take you to the Agency. You are under arrest." Sitting Bull said, "How, let me put on my clothes and go with you." He told one of his wives to get his clothes. After he had dressed, [he] arose to go and ordered his son to saddle up his horse. The police told him that it was already outside waiting for him.

> When Sitting Bull started to go with the police . . . one
> of Sitting Bull's wives burst into a loud cry which drew
> attention. No sooner had this started, when several of
> the leaders were rapidly making their way toward Sit-
> ting Bull's cabin making all sorts of complaints about the
> actions of the Indian police. The Bear That Catches, par-
> ticularly, came up close, saying "Now, here are the *ceska
> maza*—metal breasts [meaning police badges], just as we
> expected all the time. You think you are going to take
> him. You shall not do it."
> . . . By this time the whole camp was in commo-
> tion—women and children crying while the men gath-
> ered all round us—said everything mean imaginable but
> had not done anything to hurt us. The police tried to
> keep order but [it] was useless—it was like trying to ex-
> tinguish a treacherous prairie fire. Bear That Catches, in
> the heat of the excitement, pulled out a gun from under
> his blanket and fired into Lieut. Bullhead and wounded
> him.
> Lieut. Bullhead fired into Sitting Bull while still hold-
> ing him and Red Tomahawk followed with another shot
> which finished the Chief.

The melee continued, with the police, now under Red Toma-
hawk's command, taking refuge in Sitting Bull's cabin and Sitting
Bull's followers scattered around the house, firing toward and
into it. One of the policemen, Hawk Man, rode out from the camp
to Fechet's cavalry detachment. After hearing Hawk Man's report,
Fechet ordered his men forward at a gallop. Upon reaching a spot
in sight of the camp, he ordered the gunners to fire the Hotchkiss
cannon into the timber that lay between the troops and the camp.

The arrival of Fechet's troops quickly scattered Sitting Bull's
defenders. The Hunkpapa fled up the Grand River; instead of
pursuing them, Fechet ordered a messenger ahead with word that
the Indians would not be harmed if they returned peacefully.

In all, six policemen and eight of Sitting Bull's people had been
killed, including the chief as well as his 17-year-old son Crow Foot.
Sitting Bull was buried at Fort Yates, while McLaughlin arranged
a ceremonial funeral for the dead policemen at Standing Rock
Agency. With the defiant Hunkpapa leader now gone, and most

SITTING BULL'S DEATH: THE DEBATE

The death of Sitting Bull brought an outcry among many Indian-rights advocates, who suspected that Agent McLaughlin's policemen had instructions to kill the chief, rather than simply arrest him. In New York, Rev. W. H. H. Murray proclaimed "The land grabbers wanted the Indian land. The lying, thieving Indian agents wanted silence touching past thefts and immunity to continue their thieving . . . And so he was murdered."

McLaughlin himself heaped praise upon the actions of the Standing Rock police, and for the next few years campaigned for pensions for the survivors and for the families of the policemen killed at Grand River. In one letter to the Commission of Indian Affairs, he recommended to the commissioner that

> . . . a pension of at least $15 per month be given to each of the families of Bullhead, Shavehead and Little Eagle, and $10 per month to each of the families of Paul Akicitah, Hawkman No. 1, and John Armstrong, who were killed and also $10 per month to Alexander Middle, who was severely wounded and will probably lose his foot. Also that each of the 33 policemen and 4 volunteers, survivors of this engagement, receive a medal commemorative of their fidelity, and a payment at the rate of $50 per head for the ponies they had killed and those that stampeded during the fight.
>
> No information has been received that this suggestion has been acted upon or that anything has been accomplished for the relief of the parties named; and I would respectfully recommend that the matter be placed before Congress early in the approaching session.

Despite the respect McLaughlin commanded among politicians and bureaucrats in Washington, his suggestions would not be carried out. Whether through a bureaucratic oversight, or through fear of bad publicity for rewarding those labeled in the press as the murderers of Sitting Bull, the Congress never appropriated the pensions or special compensation for the Standing Rock police involved in the Grand River fight.

of the Ghost Dancers quietly surrendering at Pine Ridge Agency, the military and the agents believed they would soon have the situation under control. A violent outbreak had been avoided, and there were only a few scattered centers of the Ghost Dance remaining—a small group in the Badlands, and Big Foot's band of Miniconjou, camped in the distant plains and creek valleys on the western edge of the Cheyenne River Reservation.

NOTES

p. 65   "Buffalo Bill has arrived . . ." Commissioner of Indian Affairs, *Annual Report 1892*, p. 331.

p. 65   "Colonel Cody's capacity . . ." Smith, p. 148.

p. 66   "'Well, you're too late . . .'" Frank Bennett Fiske. *Life and Death of Sitting Bull* (Fort Yates: Pioneer Arrow Press, 1933), p. 39.

p. 66   "The order for the detention . . ." Smith, p. 149.

p. 66   "The division commander has directed . . ." Commissioner of Indian Affairs, *Annual Report 1892*, p. 333.

pp. 68–69 "We rode in a dogtrot . . ." Stanley Vestal [Walter S. Campbell] papers, Western History Collections, University of Oklahoma.

p. 70   "The land grabbers wanted . . ." *New York World*, December 21, 1890.

p. 70   " . . . a pension of at least . . ." Commissioner of Indian Affairs, *Annual Report 1892*, p. 338.

BIG FOOT'S
BAND

With Sitting Bull dead, several hundred of his followers were now fleeing from the Grand River settlement. General Miles and the colonels in command of the scattered cavalry units now feared that the angry Hunkpapa would unite with the Miniconjou of Cheyenne River, or perhaps run all the way to the Stronghold and prepare for an all-out fight with the army. To prevent any incidents, Drum recalled his troops to Fort Yates, while Agent McLaughlin sent out several messengers from his headquarters at the Standing Rock Agency. As they reached the scattered members of Sitting Bull's band, they promised the Hunkpapa that they would not be harmed if they came in to the agency immediately. About 250 of the Indians obeyed; the rest continued south, along Cherry Creek and into the Cheyenne River Reservation. Hungry and destitute, they arrived in Hump's camp on Cherry Creek or Big Foot's village of Miniconjou, who lived at the mouth of Deep Creek along the Cheyenne River.

At first one of the most defiant Lakota leaders, Hump had by this time been convinced to give up the Ghost Dance. After Thanksgiving, General Miles had ordered Captain Ezra Ewers, an acquaintance of Hump's who had known the chief for many years, to come north from his post in Texas. Ewers met with Hump on December 6 and asked the chief to give up the Ghost Dance. According to the report of the secretray of war, Hump "replied that if General Miles sent for him, he would do whatever he desired. He immediately brought his people into Fort Bennett and complied with all the orders and instructions given him, and subsequently rendered valuable service for peace." Ewers had not

In December 1890, the Lakota chiefs called on Big Foot, a skilled diplomat, to help them resolve their differences over the Ghost Dance. This mission brought Big Foot's Miniconjou band south to Pine Ridge. *(Oil painting by Henry H. Cross. From the Minnesota Historical Society)*

only persuaded the chief to bring his band in to Fort Bennett, he had also convinced Hump to enlist as a scout with the army.

Although Big Foot also had given up the Ghost Dance by this time, several members of his band still practiced it, and many of his young warriors, following his lead, remained openly hostile to the white settlers and soldiers. The Miniconjou were closely watched by the soldiers at Camp Cheyenne, which on December 3 had come under the command of Lieutenant Colonel Edwin Sumner. Taking the initiative, Sumner had met with Big Foot and the other headmen of the Miniconjou village and had found the chief friendly and willing to cooperate. Confident that the chief wanted to stay out of any confrontation with the whites, Sumner concluded that Big Foot should be allowed to lead his own people and not be harassed or arrested.

But General Miles was not feeling so confident about the Miniconjou chief. He saw Big Foot as a hostile, unyielding traditionalist, the heir to Sitting Bull as the leader of the Ghost Dance resistance. With Big Foot leading one of the largest nonprogressive bands on any of the reservations, and now attracting Ghost Dancers from among Sitting Bull's followers, Miles wanted the chief arrested and his people brought into the agency, where the army could keep a close eye on them.

On December 15, Big Foot was preparing to lead his band down the Cheyenne River and to the agency for the ration issue that would take place on the 22nd. On the 17th, the flight of the Hunkpapa after Sitting Bull's death prompted General Ruger, at the St. Paul headquarters of the Department of Dakota, to wire these instructions to Colonel Sumner: "It is desirable that Big Foot be arrested . . . In case of arrest, he will be sent to Fort Meade to be securely sent prisoner." This indirect order to capture Big Foot left the time and place for the arrest up to Colonel Sumner.

While Sumner considered his next move, Colonel H. C. Merriam, commander of the troops stationed around Fort Bennett, prepared to move the Seventh Infantry Regiment up the Cheyenne River to rendezvous with Sumner. Merriam asked Captain J. H. Hurst, commander of Fort Bennett, to send a man ahead to parlay with any Miniconjou or Hunkpapa refugees he might meet. Hurst selected Lieutenant H. E. Hale, who then rode out from Bennett with Hump. On the 20th they met the Sitting Bull fugitives at Cheyenne City, a small settlement that had been entirely deserted by its inhabitants except for one rancher. Hale asked the Hunkpapa to camp where they were and wait for Captain Hurst to ride out to their camp. Hurst met the party the next day and arranged for a feast and a council. During the council, he asked the Hunkpapa to give up their weapons and come in to Fort Bennett, where they would be safe and would be issued provisions. If they joined Big Foot, he warned, they would all be killed. Hurst persuaded most of the refugees to return with him; but 38 of the Hunkpapa rode away from the camp and into Big Foot's band.

Sumner waited until the 19th before moving against Big Foot. On that day, after hearing a report of Miniconjou plundering a white store, he ordered his command to ride east for Cherry Creek. Sumner and Miles worried that the Hunkpapa warriors who were now joining Big Foot's band at Cherry Creek would incite the Miniconjou to begin raiding white settlements and to fight the soldiers. By the time he reached Big Foot on December 21, Sumner knew that Miles expected him to arrest the chief at the first opportunity. But as tension between his own soldiers and Big Foot's warriors grew along the road to Deep Creek, Sumner decided to allow the Miniconjou and their leader to return to their village. Any attempt to arrest Big Foot, Sumner realized, would probably provoke an open fight with the band.

Big Foot, meanwhile, was pondering an invitation he had received from the Oglala chiefs at Pine Ridge Agency. Earlier in December, the chiefs had asked him to come south and help them settle their differences over the Ghost Dance. They believed that of all the Lakota chiefs, Big Foot was the most capable of resolving the crisis over the new religion and among the factions of progressive and nonprogressive Lakota. For his services, they would make him a generous gift of 100 ponies.

On December 23, Sumner decided to send his interpreter, Felix Benoit, and a rancher named John Dunn into Big Foot's camp. The two men were to persuade the chief to fulfill a promise he had previously made to Sumner and move his band east to the Cheyenne River Agency. While Sumner prepared to follow Dunn with his troops, Colonel Merriam was marching his infantry westward up the Cheyenne River to further pressure Big Foot's band to surrender.

When he reached Deep Creek, Dunn told Big Foot that the band would be attacked by Sumner's troops if it did not start out for the agency and Fort Bennett. "I am ordered to go down to Bennett tomorrow morning," Big Foot told his people. "We must all go to Bennett . . . John Dunn is sent here to tell me that if we don't go the soldiers will come here in the morning and make us go, and shoot us if they have to." But many of the other Miniconjou wanted to go to Pine Ridge. With Sumner and Merriam threatening him from both sides, Big Foot decided to bring his people out of their village and wait to see what the white soldiers did. That night, with Dunn's frightening threat in their minds, the other leaders of the band convinced the chief to move away from the soldiers, to the south, and join the other Lakota chiefs at Pine Ridge.

On December 24, Sumner received a telegram from General Miles asking that ". . . you secure Big Foot and the 20 Cheyenne River Indians, and the Standing Rock Indians, and if necessary round up the whole camp and disarm them, and take them to Fort Meade or Bennett." This, along with the surrender of Kicking Bear and Short Bull, would be the last step in ending the Ghost Dance crisis. By this time, however, Big Foot's band had slipped past the troops surrounding it and begun moving south along Deep Creek.

The army mobilized nearly every unit in the area to find Big Foot. Colonel Eugene Carr and the Sixth Cavalry, who were camped along Rapid Creek, probed eastward into the Badlands. Major Guy Henry with the Ninth Cavalry moved out from Pine Ridge Agency, searching the plateaus and hills just east of the Stronghold. The Miniconjou escaped these troops by moving directly south from their village, across the northern edge of the

Big Foot's band crossed this pass in the Badlands on their way to Wounded Knee Creek. The pass is now known as Big Foot Pass. *(Photo by Tom Streissguth)*

Badlands and down past the cliffs and dry gullies of what is now called Big Foot Pass. That same day, the band camped on White River; on Christmas Day they reached Cedar Spring, and on the next day Red Water Creek. The wagons moved slowly; Big Foot himself lay in one of them, suffering from pneumonia.

On the 26th, General Brooke learned that Big Foot's band was moving south along Porcupine Creek and heading directly for Pine Ridge Agency. The general ordered units of the Seventh Cavalry under Major Samuel Whitside out to intercept and disarm the band. On the next day, while Whitside's troops searched for the Miniconjou, the peace mission from Pine Ridge finally persuaded Kicking Bear, Short Bull, and the last hostile Ghost Dancers to leave the Stronghold.

Whitside's squadron of four cavalry troops and an artillery battery camped on Wounded Knee Creek on the night of December 26. From there, Whitside sent scouts out the next morning to search the hills to the north for Big Foot's band. Big Foot, meanwhile, decided to turn directly toward Brooke to give himself up.

HOW WOUNDED KNEE
GOT ITS NAME

In 1976, the following account of the origins of the name
Wounded Knee was written by Jim Gillihan, also known as
Tatonka Ska', or White Buffalo. At the time he was serving
as director of the Office of Cultural Preservation for the state
of South Dakota.

> Wounded Knee is located on the Pine Ridge Sioux Indian
> Reservation in southwestern South Dakota. Its name is
> derived from an event that took place at the site in the mid-
> nineteenth century. According to one version of the story, an
> Oglala was not able to provide for his wife, so she left him to
> be cared for by another man. Her original husband made every
> effort to get his wife back, but with no avail. He loved her so
> much that he gave all of his horses to her new provider and
> prepared himself to go off to die the next night. As he was
> about to leave the camp, he shot at the dogs and one of the
> arrows missed its mark and struck an old man sitting with a
> pipe. The arrow broke the man's knee cap, so the place be-
> came known as "Cankpe Opi" or shot in the knee. It was later
> translated as wounded knee.

He was too ill to move any faster and had no desire to fight with
or try to evade the soldiers.

On the morning of the 28th, four of Whitside's scouts spotted
the Miniconjou band marching from Porcupine Creek to
Wounded Knee Creek. When the scouts reached the band, Big
Foot asked two of them to return to Whitside and declare that he
intended to surrender. Instead of waiting for the band to come in,
however, Whitside ordered his men to move out immediately and
put an end to the chase. Forming opposing skirmish lines, the
soldiers and Big Foot's band finally met west of Porcupine Creek.
Through an interpreter, Whitside asked the chief to surrender
immediately and to make his camp along the banks of Wounded
Knee Creek.

At Whitside's orders, Big Foot was moved into an army ambu-
lance for the rest of the journey to Wounded Knee. Whitside also
sent a request for reinforcements by heliograph (a relay system of

signal mirrors) to the agency. Whitside believed a show of force, and the presence of the Hotchkiss cannons on a nearby hill, would discourage the Indians from any thought of resistance the next morning.

After receiving Whitside's report, Brooke ordered Colonel James Forsyth to bring the remaining four troops of the Seventh Cavalry Regiment, as well as another Hotchkiss battery, from the agency to Wounded Knee Creek. Accompanying the soldiers was a squad of Oglala scouts, under the command of Lieutenant Charles Taylor, and the interpreter Philip Wells; several newspaper reporters also followed along. Forsyth's orders were to help Whitside disarm the band and then to bring his own squadron back to the agency. Whitside would march the disarmed Miniconjou directly from Wounded Knee Creek south to the rail stop at Gordon, Nebraska, where they would be placed on a train for a prison in Omaha.

The reinforcements from Pine Ridge arrived late on the evening of December 28. In all, 27 officers, 433 enlisted men, and about 30

Officers of the Seventh Cavalry and their wives gather at Pine Ridge Agency before the fight at Wounded Knee. *(South Dakota State Historical Society, Pierre)*

scouts camped just south of the village of Wounded Knee. The Miniconjou numbered about 120 men and 230 women and children. Big Foot lay in a tent between the cavalry camp and his band, which camped to the south near a dry ravine that ran east to the creek. Overlooking the site to the west was a small hill, where the artillery troops positioned the four Hotchkiss guns.

The sun went down early. In the morning, Forsyth and Whitside would disarm Big Foot's followers, and the last hostile Indian leader would be on his way to a prison. The Ghost Dance War would be over; the Lakota would finally have to accept the tide of white civilization that had already swept across every other nation of the Plains Indians.

NOTES

pp. 72–73 "replied that if . . ." Mooney, p. 862.

p. 74 "It is desirable . . ." Utley, p. 175.

p. 76 "I am ordered . . ." Utley, p. 183.

p. 78 "Wounded Knee is located . . ." Jim Gillihan manuscript, *How Wounded Knee Got Its Name, and Related Historic Incidents,* South Dakota State Archives.

7

"FIRE! FIRE ON THEM!"

Early in the clear and warm morning of December 29, the scout Louis Shangreau walked across the open field that lay between the tents of the Seventh Cavalry and the tipis of Big Foot's Miniconjou village. Shangreau carried a message from Colonel Forsyth: Big Foot and the Miniconjou warriors must assemble in the square for a council.

Forsyth had already positioned his troops around the meeting ground. He intended to surround the Indians with hundreds of dismounted cavalrymen, who would form up in lines and stand facing the Indians like soldiers standing at attention in a military parade ground. Dismounted, the men of Troops B and K took their places to the west and south, respectively, of the square. These troops stood between the Miniconjou men at the council and the women and children who would remain in the Indians' camp. G Troop, mounted, took its place across the agency road to the east. Troops A and I were spread out farther west, with most of the men dismounted and forming a thin line across the small ravine that lay south of the Miniconjou village. On the hills beyond the ravine were Colonel Taylor's Oglala scouts; C and D troops, also mounted, formed up behind the scouts. E Troop watched from one of the hills to the west. On the other, higher hill, now known as Cemetery Hill, stood the two Hotchkiss batteries, with four cannons. There was no road for escape, nor was there any hope for an even fight, if the Miniconjou should think of resisting Forsyth's orders.

Shangreau announced to Big Foot that the colonel wanted to disarm the band's warriors. To prevent any trouble on the march that was to come, the Miniconjou must surrender their rifles. Shangreau advised Big Foot to agree to the order, reminding the chief that the band could get more guns, if needed, but could never replace warriors killed in a fight. Big Foot considered and then instructed his men to give up their older, least useful guns. That might satisfy the colonel, and the band would not be left completely defenseless.

Colonel Forsyth and Major Whitside counted off 20 warriors and sent them to the Miniconjou camp to bring back the weapons. After a short time, the Indians returned with two old carbines, shorter-barreled guns that the Lakotas had long given up in favor of the longer, more accurate Winchester rifles. Realizing that Big Foot and the Miniconjou were stalling, Forsyth then ordered the chief to come out of his tent. Big Foot, still too ill to walk, was carried out and placed on the ground between his own warriors and the formidable line of cavalry officers and enlisted men. Forsyth again demanded that the Indians give up all their guns, but Big Foot insisted there were no more. The band, he claimed, had already surrendered all of their good rifles at the Cheyenne River Agency.

Colonel Forsyth knew that Big Foot was lying—he had seen the Miniconjou carrying their Winchester rifles the day before, during the surrender. He ordered two details of 15 men each from B and K troops to enter the Indian village. Enlisted men were to search the wagons and grounds outside the tipis. Captain George Wallace and Lieutenant James Mann of K Troop, Captain Charles Varnum of B Troop, and Lieutenant Ernest Garlington would search the tipis. The two groups worked toward each other from opposite ends of the village. While the enlisted men rummaged through the Miniconjou wagons, the officers in the tipis found guns hidden under blankets, inside the flaps of the tipis, and under the skirts of the Miniconjou women. The officers passed ammunition and weapons, including guns, knives, and bows and arrows, out to the enlisted men. "The squaws were sitting on bundles concealing guns and other arms," Lieutenant Mann wrote. "The squaws made no resistance, and when we took the arms they seemed to be satisfied." Some of the weapons were placed in the tents of the scouts; others were loaded on wagons and moved away from the council grounds.

As their weapons were taken away, the Miniconjou warriors grew restless. Determined to resist this humiliation, they began to mill about the meeting ground, holding their rifles close and ready underneath their blankets. The cavalrymen standing around the square gripped their own weapons and watched for any sudden or threatening movements. A Miniconjou medicine man named Yellow Bird began dancing around the square, gesturing at the white soldiers and urging the warriors to resist. Yellow Bird promised that the Ghost Shirts they were wearing would protect the Indians from harm. "That man is making mischief," Philip Wells remarked to Forsyth. Through Wells, Forsyth ordered Yellow Bird to sit down. The medicine man did so and for a short time fell silent.

The search of the village had turned up several good rifles, but not enough, Forsyth was sure, to account for all the Miniconjou arms. The colonel demanded that the warriors come forward immediately to surrender their guns. A few of the band stepped away from the group and threw off their blankets, revealing no weapons. The others stood in place, not moving or responding. Major Whitside and Captain Varnum then began searching the Indians one by one. They found rifles and ammunition; a sergeant held Varnum's hat while the captain emptied cartridges into it. The Miniconjou began to move to the east, toward the agency road and away from the cavalry lines. "Be ready," said Lieutenant Mann to the men of K Troop, on the southern edge of the council ground. "There is going to be trouble."

One of the warriors, Black Coyote, was holding his rifle out above his head for all to see. He would not give up his gun, he shouted, without being paid for it. Two cavalrymen grabbed Black

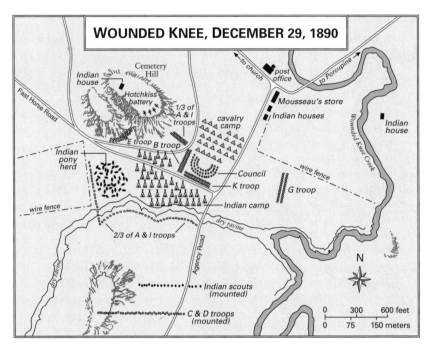

White troops and Indian scouts were positioned around Big Foot's band in an attempt by Seventh Cavalry officers to ensure a peaceful surrender.

Coyote from behind and began wrestling with him. The Indian's rifle rose into the air and went off. Yellow Bird, who had begun speaking and gesturing again, threw a handful of dirt into the air; a group of Miniconjou then threw off their blankets, leveled their rifles at K Troop, and fired a volley at the soldiers.

Lieutenant Mann gave the order: "Fire! Fire on them!" Standing perhaps a dozen yards distant, K Troop, from the south, and B Troop, on the west side, fired directly into the Indians on the eastern edge of the council grounds. Bullets flew across the square in all directions as the troops positioned on the edges of the meeting ground fired toward the center. Big Foot and the other band chiefs near him were killed immediately. Captain Wallace, rushing back toward K Troop, died from a shot to the head—a shot which may have come from a cavalryman's gun.

Most of the warriors rushed toward the Miniconjou camp lying just past the line of soldiers. Others broke across the road toward

G Troop. The cavalrymen and the Miniconjou fought at close range with knives and revolvers. A slashing knife nearly took away Philip Wells's nose; one of the reporters at the scene took up a gun and began firing at the Indians. Colonel Forsyth fled the square and raced up to the Hotchkiss battery, commanded by Captain Allyn Capron. As the warriors broke away from the square, the men of B and K troops moved back, toward the cavalry camp. Unable to distinguish friendly cavalry from the Indians, Capron had held his fire until the melee ended and the two sides had separated. Now, with the gunners aiming for the small groups of scattering Indians, all four guns opened fire at once.

The shells streamed across the battlefield and toward the Miniconjou village. Shrapnel sprayed into the tipis, several of which began burning. Terrified, the Miniconjou women grabbed their children and ran for the shallow, dry ravine that cut behind the camp. The warriors followed them, drawing fire from the line of

After the fighting broke out between Big Foot's warriors and the Seventh Cavalry, Miniconjou women and children took shelter in this dry ravine just south of the battlefield. A bombardment from the Hotchkiss battery killed many of them. *(Photo by Tom Streissguth)*

dismounted soldiers of A and I troops who stood on the ravine's opposite edge. As the Miniconjou fled west and east along the ravine, the Hotchkiss crews began training their guns on the ditch. Shells exploded against the ravine walls and bottom, killing men, women, and children.

A small group broke away to the west, following the ravine in a desperate search for shelter. The Oglala scouts scattered, while C and D troops formed skirmish lines and advanced. Troop E moved down from its hill and into the ravine. The Miniconjou who were still fighting in the ravine faced hostile units shooting back from nearly all sides. A Brulé named Turning Hawk later testified that

> [the men] who escaped that first fire got into the ravine, and as they went along up the ravine they were pursued on both sides by the soldiers and shot down . . . The women were standing off at a different place from where the men were stationed, and when the firing began, those of the men who escaped the first onslaught went in one direction up the ravine, and then the women, who were bunched together at another place, went entirely in a different direction through an open field, and the women fared the same fate as the men who went up the deep ravine.

The ravine had become a death trap for dozens of Miniconjou women and their children; desperately digging for shelter in the cold ground, the women were cut down by the rapid-fire Hotchkiss guns that were raining shells down from Cemetery Hill.

Indian men, women, and ponies then broke away from the ravine and began running toward the agency road. The soldiers of C and D troops opened fire on the fleeing group, killing them singly and in groups. Another group of Miniconjou fled several hundred yards to the west, where men, women, and children collected in the shelter of a sharp bend. Here a group of about 25 warriors kept up the last resistance, exchanging fire with several units until a group of scouts advanced and negotiated a cease-fire. In the meantime, Philip Wells had rushed up to the edge of the ravine and called out: "All of you who are still alive, give up and come on over, you will not be molested or shot at any more." Some of the wounded raised themselves and began to climb past the bodies scattered on the ravine's slopes.

The bodies of Miniconjou warriors and soldiers of K and B troops lay around the battlefield. Big Foot and his fellow chiefs lay dead, along with more than 100 Miniconjou men, women, and children. Father Francis Craft, a Catholic priest who had been present at the disarming, began giving last rites to the dying, even after suffering a stab wound that collapsed one of his lungs. The cavalry soldiers placed the wounded on wagons, and the regiment marched the 15 miles back to Pine Ridge Agency. A church there served as a field hospital, managed by Dr. Charles Eastman. " . . . we laid the poor creatures side by side in rows, and the night was devoted to caring for them as best we could. Many were frightfully torn by pieces of shells, and the suffering was terrible." The Indian women, terrified by the site of the blue uniforms, would not allow the army surgeons to approach them.

The gunfire at Wounded Knee carried across the hills and plains of the Pine Ridge Reservation. One settler recalls hearing the shots, then riding in to the agency to seek permission to leave in search of his brother.

> I waited on Brooke—he said [sic] I could go if I wanted to, but in his opinion, I was taking ten chances to my brother's one. When I first spoke of the fight he seemed surprised. *"What fight, sir, what excitement?* I know of no excitement only what is here in the Agency." Just then as he paused, boom-boom-boom! Muffled and indistinct, but still unmistakably cannon shots. The old man coloured slightly and said "Even granted that they are fighting at W.K. I have men enough there to eat them up. What danger do you fear for your brother?" "Just this, General, no matter which way the fight goes, there may be stragglers get away, and they are as liable to go one way as another."
>
> "I tell you again, Sir, I don't propose to have any stragglers get away! *Go if you want to.*" And I didn't hesitate,

but went quick, and I think from the way Brooke looked,
it was the best thing I could do just then.

Hearing the noise, the Oglala and Brulé at the agency began to
panic, fearing a general massacre that would bring death to their
own camps as well. Elaine Goodale Eastman recalled that "Their
white camps melted away like snow-banks in April. The brown
hills were instantly alive with galloping horsemen and a long line
of loaded wagons disappeared in the distance." Others prepared
to fight. The followers of Little Wound, No Water, Short Bull,
Kicking Bear, Big Road, and Red Cloud left their campsites near
the agency and scattered to the valley of White Clay Creek, on the
way north to the now-abandoned Stronghold.

On the streets of Pine Ridge, the warriors of Two Strike's Brulé
band began firing at the Indian police. The police took up position
in the agency streets and returned the fire, while Dr. Charles
Eastman watched:

> Just then General Brooke ran out into the open, shouting
> at the top of his voice to the police: "Stop! Stop! Doctor,
> tell them they must not fire until ordered!" I did so, as
> the bullets whistled by us, and the General's coolness
> perhaps saved all our lives, for we were in no position to
> repel a large attacking force. Since we did not reply, the
> scattered shots ceased, but the situation remained criti-
> cal for several days and nights.

The shooting at the agency died down, but scattered fighting
continued around the reservation. A wagon train of the Ninth
Cavalry was attacked on its way north to the agency with supplies;
several houses were burned along the road to the Holy Rosary
Catholic Mission, also called the Drexel Mission, which lay a few
miles northwest of the agency. Miles and Brooke had expected a
peaceful settlement of the Ghost Dance War; instead the reservation was sliding into an all-out war.

On the next day, Brooke ordered Colonel Forsyth to bring his
troops the few miles out of the agency to Drexel Mission, the home
of Father Jutz, who had helped negotiate the surrender of Kicking

Bear and Short Bull in the Badlands. Forsyth's orders were to drive off any Lakota who might be attacking the mission and bring Jutz and the other missionaries in to the agency. Jutz believed he was in no danger, as the Lakota, who liked and respected him, had sent word that morning that he and his mission would be safe. Now, while Forsyth marched toward Drexel Mission with four cavalry troops and a Hotchkiss gun, Jutz and his colleagues were taking shelter within the mission with a group of frightened refugees.

After reaching the mission, and finding it quiet, Forsyth turned his men north, along White Clay Creek, where he believed a fight between hostile Indians and a cavalry unit was taking place. Forsyth led his men into a valley lined on both sides by steep ridges. Lakota warriors quickly took up position along the bluff tops and began firing on Forsyth's troops. The colonel was trapped, unable to advance farther down the valley or to retreat to the south, where other warriors had opened fire. He sent a messenger back to ask for help from the Ninth Cavalry under Major Guy Henry, whose troops were camped at Pine Ridge Agency. The Ninth arrived in about half an hour and rescued the colonel, who lost two men as a result of the skirmish.

A storm started later that day and blew across the Wounded Knee battlefield for two days. On New Year's Eve a burial detail, commanded by Lieutenant George W. Kirkman, was sent out from Pine Ridge Agency. After reaching the battlefield, the workers spent a day and a half collecting the bodies of the Miniconjou dead onto horse-drawn wagons, discovering as they worked that a few of the wounded Indians were still alive after surviving three days in the open during a blizzard. The detail brought the bodies up to Cemetery Hill, the site of the Hotchkiss battery that had fired down onto the battlefield three days before. In the cold and silence the men dug a mass grave 60 feet long and six feet deep, then threw Big Foot and more than 100 of his people into the pit. Before the burial many of the bodies were stripped of clothing, jewelry, and ghost shirts.

A five-foot chain-link fence now surrounds the grave, which is topped by a squat stone marker commemorating the "Big Foot

On New Year's Day, Big Foot and more than 100 members of his band were dumped without ceremony into a mass grave. *(Photo by Northwestern Photo Co. From the Minnesota Historical Society)*

Fight." The names of some, not all, of the Miniconjou who died at Wounded Knee are carved on the stone. Visitors to the site lean on the fence, contemplating the long grave, the battlefield lying at the foot of the hill to the east, and the needless, violent deaths of so many people. The hill and the monument look out over the site of the last, desperate fight of the Lakota against the civilization that was sweeping their traditional way of life aside.

Instead of ending the Ghost Dance peacefully, the deployment of the military to the Lakota reservations had brought about a massacre. The grieving and bitterness caused by Wounded Knee continues to the present day, as the Lakota descendants of the victims and the U.S. government contend over a new memorial to mark the site, over medals awarded to men of the Seventh Cavalry, and over compensation from the government for treaties broken and land stolen.

DR. EASTMAN TREATS
THE WOUNDED

Dr. Charles Eastman was a Santee Dakota who spent eight years of his youth living among the whites and learning their science and medicine. Determined to use his training as a doctor to serve the Indians he had left behind on the reservations, he returned to the Great Plains and was hired as agency doctor at Pine Ridge in the summer of 1890.

Dr. Eastman arrived while the Ghost Dance movement was sweeping the Lakota reservations. On December 28, he witnessed Colonel Forsyth's Seventh Cavalry squadron leave the agency to take part in the disarmament of Big Foot's band at Wounded Knee Creek. A few days after the massacre, once the storm had subsided, Eastman volunteered to set out with a rescue party, including about 100 Indians and white civilians, to look for survivors. In his book, *From the Deep Woods to Civilization: Chapters in the Autobiography of an Indian*, Eastman described what he saw at Wounded Knee:

> Fully three miles from the scene of the massacre we found the body of a woman completely covered with a blanket of snow, and from this point on we found them scattered along as they had been relentlessly hunted down and slaughtered while fleeing for their lives. Some of our people discovered relatives or friends among the dead, and there was much wailing and mourning. When we reached the spot where the Indian camp had stood, among the fragments of burned tents and other belongings we saw the frozen bodies lying close together or piled one upon another. I counted eighty bodies of men who had been in the council and who were almost as helpless as the women and babes when the deadly fire began, for nearly all their guns had been taken from them. . . .
>
> All this was a severe ordeal for one who had so lately put his faith in the Christian love and lofty ideals of the white man.

After Wounded Knee, Turning Hawk was called on by the U.S. Congress to tell what he had seen and done during the Wounded Knee fight.

I stood very loyal to the government all through those troublesome days, and believing so much in the government and being so loyal to it, my disappointment was very strong . . . the fact of the killing of the women, and more especially the killing of the young boys and girls who are to go to make up the future strength of the Indian people, is the saddest part of the whole affair and we feel it very sorely.

NOTES

p. 83   "The squaws were sitting . . ." Utley, pp. 209–210.

p. 86   "[the men] who escaped . . ." Commissioner of Indian Affairs, *Annual Report 1892*, p. 180.

p. 87   ". . . we laid the poor creatures . . ." Dr. Charles A. Eastman, p. 110.

pp. 87–88 "I waited on Brooke . . ." O. R. Ainsworth manuscript, South Dakota State Archives.

p. 88   "Their white camps . . ." Elaine Goodale Eastman, p. 36.

p. 88   "Just then General Brooke . . ." Dr. Charles A. Eastman, p. 108.

p. 91   "Fully three miles . . ." Matthieson, pp. 20–21.

p. 92   "I stood very loyal . . ." Commissioner of Indian Affairs, *Annual Report 1892*, p. 181.

AFTERWORD

▲

U nder the direction of its pas-
tor, Rev. Charles Cook, the
Episcopal chapel at Pine Ridge Agency was turned into a field
hospital. The pews were torn out; hay was spread over the floor
to provide bedding for the dying and the wounded. At least 30
Lakota men and women lay on the floor, brought in by the Seventh

A burial detail collected the dead at Wounded Knee. *(Photo by George Trager.
From the Minnesota Historical Society)*

The Ghost Dance leader Kicking Bear talks to a meeting of Lakota at Pine Ridge after Wounded Knee. *(South Dakota State Historical Society, Pierre)*

Cavalry on the night of December 29. Dr. Eastman and his aides tended as best they could to the bullet wounds and broken bones. Most of his patients died within a few days.

General Miles, meanwhile, had arrived at Pine Ridge Agency from his headquarters at Rapid City. He sent out a message to Kicking Bear, Short Bull, and other Oglala and Brulé chiefs who had fled the agency after the fight: "You know that I did what was right by you before; I shall do what is right by you now. I must be Chief. I know I can do you good. If you expect me to help you, you must help me by doing what I want you to do." He wanted the chiefs to surrender, to come to the agency, and lay down their weapons.

Miles and Brooke had brought outlying units closer to Pine Ridge Reservation, gradually drawing in the ring of soldiers surrounding the reservation. Scattered encounters continued during the first two weeks of January, until January 15, when Kicking Bear and Short Bull again brought their followers in from White Clay Creek. Miles arranged to have the two Ghost Dance leaders, as well as 20 of their warriors, held as hostages to prevent any more trouble. The Indians were placed on a train bound for Fort Sheridan, Illinois, near Chicago.

General Miles's plan to arrest Big Foot, disarm his band, and thus put a quiet end to the Ghost Dance hostilities had failed. The disarmament of Big Foot's Miniconjou had turned into a fierce, close-range battle and then a massacre of innocent women and children. As many as 200 Miniconjou and 34 officers and enlisted men of the U.S. Cavalry had died at Wounded Knee, and many more died later of their wounds or died in the fighting that took place in the following days. Miles blamed Colonel Sumner, for allowing Big Foot to flee from the Cheyenne River Reservation, and Colonel Forsyth, for mishandling the disarming of the band on the morning of the 29th. On January 4, Forsyth was relieved of his command; under Miles's direction a court of inquiry was convened. Jacob Ford Kent, inspector general of the Division of the Missouri, and Captain Frank Baldwin, assistant inspector general, were put in charge of the investigation.

Lakota Indians make camp at Pine Ridge after the tragedy at Wounded Knee. *(South Dakota State Historical Society, Pierre)*

MURDER AND JUSTICE IN
EARLY SOUTH DAKOTA

In the weeks following the Wounded Knee massacre, violent confrontations and killings continued in western South Dakota, both on and off the reservations. On January 7, Lieutenant Edward Casey, an officer of the 22nd Infantry Regiment and the leader of a squad of Cheyenne scouts, was traveling in the Pine Ridge Reservation with two of his scouts. Casey believed he could ease the tense situation by meeting and talking with the hostile Lakota who were still camping away from Pine Ridge Agency.

Casey set out on January 7 and soon met a Lakota party near White Clay Creek. He sent a messenger to Red Cloud, who was camped nearby, asking to speak with the chief or with one of his companions. In a short time, the lieutenant encountered two Brulé, Broken Arm and Plenty Horses, and then Pete Richard, an English-speaking relative of Red Cloud. Richard brought word that the Oglala chief would meet with General Miles soon and that Casey should leave the area immediately. Deciding not to insist, Casey turned his horse around just as a shot from a Winchester rifle struck him in the head, instantly killing him. After firing the shot, Plenty Horses fled the scene; the rest of the party scattered.

Three days later, two Oglala families were starting out from their camp on the Belle Fourche River, off their home reservation of Pine Ridge. Agent Daniel Royer had issued a pass to the group to leave the reservation for a hunt. Suddenly, shots rang out from the guns of three white ranchers who were hiding behind a nearby hill. Few Tails, one of the Oglala, fell dead; bullets dropped both horses pulling his wagon, and his wife, Clown, fell to the ground with two bullet wounds. In the other wagon, One Feather turned the reins over to his wife while he mounted a pony, fending off the

At the inquest, however, Forsyth's junior officers would not directly criticize their commander's deployment, testifying instead that Forsyth and his officers had not been expecting a fight. Enlisted men and officers also testified that in the smoke and attackers as the family's wagon bounced over the plains. Finally giving up the wagon, One Feather placed his wife on his own pony and his two daughters on another and rode hard for the safety of Pine Ridge Agency.

Mounting one of the horses, which was still alive, Clown rode for seven nights, while hiding during the day, over the dry plains and through the Badlands. After traveling more than 100 miles, she finally reached Pine Ridge Agency, nearly dead from her bullet wounds, hunger, and cold.

The killings of both Lieutenant Casey and Few Tails resulted in murder trials. Claiming they had surprised a party of Indians raiding their horses, the Culbertson brothers, Cheyenne River ranchers, pled innocent to the charge of killing Few Tails. But an investigation by Lieutenant F. C. Marshall showed that the Culbertsons had ambushed the Few Tails party.

General Miles turned the case of Lieutenant Casey's killing over to the state of South Dakota and then ordered the arrest of Plenty Horses on February 18. The court met in Deadwood; V. T. McGillycuddy served as jury foreman. At the grand jury hearing in Deadwood, Plenty Horses said: "Five years I attended Carlisle and was educated in the ways of the white man. When I returned to my people I was an outcast among them . . . I shot the lieutenant so I might make a place for myself among my people . . ." Pleny Horses remained in custody to await his trial that spring in Sioux Falls. Although Plenty Horses freely admitted that he killed Lieutenant Casey, the trial judge ruled that the jury could not find Plenty Horses guilty of murder, as a state of war existed on Pine Ridge Reservation. Plenty Horses was freed.

Soon after this decision, a jury in Sturgis, South Dakota, reached its decision in the murder trial of the Culbertsons. Although the white men provided no excuse for shooting Few Tails, aside from their dislike of reservation Indians, they were also found innocent of murder.

confusion of battle, they had been unable to distinguish the Miniconjou women and children from the men. On January 13, the court simply censured Forsyth for the deployment of troops at Wounded Knee, dropping the rest of the charges against him.

Seeing his own reputation tarnished by the fight, Miles made every effort to see that blame for it fell squarely on Forsyth's shoulders. Unsatisfied with the mild rebuke given on the 13th, he ordered the case reopened on January 16, three days after Baldwin and Kent wrote their opinions. This time, the court was directed to investigate whether Forsyth had obeyed Miles's explicit and repeated orders not to allow the troops to mingle with the Indians. This time, Baldwin and Kent wrote more critical judgments of Forsyth. On January 31, Miles wrote a scathing denunciation of Forsyth in his own endorsement of the court's findings.

The mass grave of Big Foot's band now overlooks the site of the Wounded Knee massacre from Cemetery Hill. *(Photo by Tom Streissguth)*

COMMEMORATING
WOUNDED KNEE

In 1990, on the 100th anniversary of Wounded Knee, Congress passed a resolution that read in part:

> (1) the Congress, on the occasion of the one hundredth anniversary of the Wounded Knee Massacre of December 29, 1890,

But Miles's own superiors, General John Schofield and Secretary of War Redfield Proctor, sought to wash their hands of the blood spilled at Wounded Knee. Proctor reinstated Forsyth, despite Miles's recommendation that the colonel be court-martialed for incompetence. Forsyth was also cleared of Miles's condemnation for incompetence in the handling of the Drexel Mission fight.

At the same time, Miles was campaigning for military control of the Lakota reservations. The controversy over the best way to manage the reservations turned into a full-scale bureaucratic war, with the Interior Department jealously guarding its privilege as

hereby acknowledges the historical significance of the event as the last armed conflict of the Indian wars period resulting in the tragic death and injury of approximately 350–375 Indian men, women, and children of Chief Big Foot's band of Minneconjou Sioux and hereby expresses its deep regret on behalf of the United States to the descendants of the victims and survivors and their respective tribal communities . . .

(2) the Congress also . . . expresses its support for the establishment of a suitable and appropriate Memorial to those who were so tragically slain at Wounded Knee which could inform the American public of the historic significance of the events at Wounded Knee and accurately portray the heroic and courageous campaign waged by the Sioux people. . . .

By acknowledging and accepting responsibility for the massacre, the resolution met one of the demands that have been made by Wounded Knee survivors and their families. But one issue that has not yet been resolved is the proper way to mark the site of Wounded Knee. The modern visitor to the Wounded Knee battlefield sees only a signboard, faded by many years of weather, and behind it an empty, barren field. At the top of a nearby hill a granite marker sits over the mass grave of the victims. Some Lakota leaders would like to see the site become a national monument, thus placing it under the authority of the National Park Service. Although many promises have been made by congressional representatives to provide money for a more fitting memorial to Wounded Knee, the promises have not yet been fulfilled.

THE WOUNDED KNEE MEMORIAL AND PINE RIDGE TODAY

One hundred years after Wounded Knee, an economic and political division remains among the Oglala Lakota and the people of the Pine Ridge Reservation. This division goes back to the earliest encounters of the United States and the Lakota in the early 19th century. Since that time, "traditional" Lakota seeking to preserve their religion and culture have opposed any compromise with the whites, while the faction called "progressive" by historians still seeks compromise and accommodation with the federal government.

The modern village of Wounded Knee lies just west of the massacre site of 1890. The tree-lined hills and buttes of this region gave the Pine Ridge Reservation its name.   *(Photo by Tom Streissguth)*

the office responsible for Indian affairs. While the Lakota and their lands were still under martial law, Miles appointed officers and gave them instructions to assume many of the responsibilities of the civilian agents. These officers included Captain E. F. Pierce, who replaced Daniel Royer at Pine Ridge; Captain Joseph Hurst at Cheyenne River; and Captain Jesse Lee at Rosebud. Determined as well as competent, James McLaughlin held firmly to his post and his authority at Standing Rock.

One important issue that is now dividing these two camps is a proposed Wounded Knee National Tribal Park. According to proposed legislation, the park would include the 1890 massacre site as well as the cemetery and mass grave that adjoins this area to the west, lying atop Cemetery Hill. A visitors' center would be built; roads that pass through the site rerouted; modern structures removed; and replicas of buildings that stood in 1890 raised. A "Chief Big Foot National Historic Trail" would commemorate the flight of Big Foot's Miniconjou band from the Cheyenne River Reservation south to the Badlands and Wounded Knee.

Traditional Lakota oppose the park as it is proposed, while the "nontraditional" faction supports it. Nontraditional Lakota believe the park would bring increased tourism; traditionals oppose placing the land in federal trust and taking it out of reservation jurisdiction. They want the land preserved as it is, and the gravesites undisturbed by construction and demolition.

In an article posted by the traditionals on the Wounded Knee World Wide Web site, Wanbli Sapa and William Cooper write,

> . . . the Congressional Delegation from South Dakota and its supporters have proposed legislation to Congress that could create a new national park at Wounded Knee on the Pine Ridge Sioux Reservation, South Dakota. Though the act is supported by a few Lakota, it is adamantly opposed by a large number of other Lakota. Those who support it stand to make financial gains. Those who oppose it stand to lose their land, and/or are deeply concerned that this site, sacred to the Lakota people, will be taken from them and their access to it denied. This concern is based on real experience, and one has only to look west a short distance to the Black Hills or north an even shorter distance to Badlands National Park, both sacred sites for the Lakota Nation, to see the reality of the concern.

Miles wanted his appointed officers to act as Indian supervisors as well as military commanders. According to his orders of January 12, the officers should

> ascertain to what extent the Indians are occupied, and whether or not rations are sufficient. . . . [officers] will ascertain and report what additional occupation could be afforded these people on the reservation, or in the immediate vicinity, and also whether means of occupa-

tion cannot be devised and developed in addition to
agriculture and pastoral pursuits . . .

These orders caused continuing controversy until a military reorganization that took place in July 1891 abolished the Division of the Missouri and stripped Miles of his command of the Department of Dakota. The Lakota reservations soon returned to entirely civilian rule, overseen by the Bureau of Indian Affairs and the Interior Department, the agencies that still hold responsibility for the government's reservation policies.

The Ghost Dance was dead, denied even by its prophet, Wovoka. But the fighting and bloodshed on the reservations convinced the U.S. government to honor some of the many broken promises of the Crook Commission and of the treaties and agreements signed over the years with the Lakota. President Harrison signed a bill that appropriated $200,000 to repay the Indians for ponies lost or stolen during the Custer campaign; $165,000 for new Indian schools on the reservations; and $100,000 to bring the annual appropriation for rations up to the previous level of $1 million a year. Later Congress also appropriated $100,000 to compensate Lakota who had lost property during the Ghost Dance troubles at Pine Ridge.

The collision of the Teton Lakota bands and the U.S. government had lasted many years—from the tense confrontation of Lewis and Clark with Black Buffalo's band in 1804 until the surrender of the Ghost Dance leaders in January 1891. The conflict was characterized by fear and misunderstanding, aggravated by the inability of the United States to honor its own treaties and the Lakota's reluctance to abandon a traditional culture forged by many generations of hunting, fighting, and wandering on the Great Plains.

Now the Lakota were confined to their six small and barren reservations, and the Great Plains frontier was closed. The spring of 1891 passed peacefully; the U.S. Cavalry had seen its last action against the Plains Indians. The Ghost Dance religion was forgotten. Short Bull and Kicking Bear, the leading apostles among the Lakota, left the reservations to join Buffalo Bill Cody's Wild West

A group of Dakota chiefs ride horseback during a peaceful gathering in 1896. *(From the Minnesota Historical Society)*

MENDING THE SACRED HOOP, 100 YEARS LATER

Before dawn on the morning of December 15, 1990, a group of Lakota Indians met for a ceremony near the Grand River on the Standing Rock Indian Reservation. The group would mark the 100th anniversary of the death of Sitting Bull, on the spot where the chief had been killed by reservation police. After the ceremony, about 50 riders set out on horseback for the 200-mile voyage to the site of Wounded Knee on the Pine Ridge Reservation.

The Lakota called the rides, which had taken place each of the previous four years, "Mending the Sacred Hoop." The five annual rides were not just a commemoration. They were an attempt to lessen and heal the divisions that have torn the Lakota Nation since well before Wounded Knee took place. A South Dakota writer named Patrick Cudmore, who lived and worked among the Oglala Lakota, explained that "The ride has been a prayer and a sacrifice, a wiping away the tears of the mourners. This year's ride, the fifth and final, was a celebration of unity and life."

Show. The elaborate movements and rituals of the dance survived only in the form of songs and games performed among the Kiowa and other tribes of the southern Plains. Wounded Knee became the bitter memory that still hangs over the Oglala's reservation and over the hills and ravines lying northeast of the small town of Pine Ridge.

NOTES

p. 94   "You know that . . ." Robert Wooster. *Nelson A. Miles and the Twilight of the Frontier Army* (Lincoln: University of Nebraska Press, 1993), p. 187.

p. 97   "Five years I attended . . ." Julia McGillycuddy. *McGilly-cuddy: Agent* (Palo Alto, Calif.: Stanford University Press, 1941), p. 272.

p. 99   "ascertain to what extent . . ." Utley, p. 280.

p. 103   "The ride has been . . ." Patrick Cudmore, "The Great American Holocaust," *Lakota Times*, January 8, 1991.

SELECTED BIBLIOGRAPHY AND FURTHER READING

Axelrod, Alan. *Chronicle of the Indian Wars*. New York: Prentice Hall, 1993. Detailed and richly illustrated survey of Indian conflicts, from the 17th century to Wounded Knee.

Bailey, Paul. *Wovoka, the Indian Messiah*. Los Angeles: Westernlore Press, 1957. An account of Wovoka's life and of the Ghost Dance faith he founded.

Brown, Dee. *Bury My Heart at Wounded Knee*. New York: Holt, Rinehart & Winston, 1970. The best-selling history of conflict between Indians and whites in North America, with a final chapter on the Wounded Knee massacre.

Eastman, Dr. Charles A. *From the Deep Woods to Civilization: Chapters in the Autobiography of an Indian*. 1916. Reprint, Lincoln: University of Nebraska Press, 1977. Autobiographical sketches of the Pine Ridge Agency doctor who witnessed the Ghost Dance movement and the aftermath of Wounded Knee.

———. *The Soul of the Indian*. Boston: Houghton Mifflin Company, 1911. An interpretation of Indian culture and religion by a doctor who lived in both the Indian and white worlds.

Green, Jerry, ed. *After Wounded Knee: Correspondence of Major and Surgeon John Vance Lauderdale while Serving with the Army Occupying the Pine Ridge Indian Reservation, 1890–91*. East Lansing: Michigan State University Press, 1996. Letters of a surgeon stationed at Pine Ridge just after the Wounded Knee massacre.

Hall, Philip S. *To Have This Land: The Nature of Indian/White Relations, South Dakota, 1888–1891*. Vermilion: University of South Dakota Press, 1991. Vividly describes and documents attitudes of white settlers and townspeople toward the Lakota during the Ghost Dance troubles.

Hyde, George E. *Red Cloud's Folk: A History of the Oglala Sioux Indians*. Norman: University of Oklahoma Press, 1931. A detailed history of the Oglala Lakota, from their migration westward in the 17th century to the late 1800s.

McGillycuddy, Julia. *McGillycuddy: Agent*. Palo Alto, Calif.: Stanford University Press, 1941. A description of the life and times of Valentine McGillycuddy, army doctor and Pine Ridge agent, written by his daughter.

Mooney, James. *The Ghost Dance Religion and the Sioux Outbreak of 1890*. Lincoln: University of Nebraska Press, 1991. A scientific study of the origins and practice of the Ghost Dance among the mountain and Plains tribes. Originally published in 1896 by the Bureau of Ethnology.

Smith, Rex Alan. *Moon of Popping Trees: The Tragedy of Wounded Knee and the End of the Indian Wars*. Lincoln: University of Nebraska Press, 1975. A popular history of the Ghost Dance troubles, including fictionalized dialogue and quotes from many primary sources.

Utley, Robert M. *The Lance and the Shield: The Life and Times of Sitting Bull*. New York: Ballantine Books, 1993. Biography of the famous Hunkpapa chief.

———. *The Last Days of the Sioux Nation*. New Haven: Yale University Press, 1963. A thoroughly researched book on the conflict of the Lakota Indians and the United States, leading up to a detailed account of the Wounded Knee massacre.

Wooster, Robert. *Nelson A. Miles and the Twilight of the Frontier Army*. Lincoln: University of Nebraska Press, 1993. Study of Miles's career and the workings of the late 19th-century U.S. Army.

INDEX

Italic page numbers indicate illustrations.
The letter *m* following a page number indicates a map.